W9-CDJ-992

How To Heal
A Painful
Relationship

AND IF NECESSARY
HOW TO PART
AS FRIENDS

Other Books by Bill Ferguson

Heal the Hurt that Runs Your Life
Discover and Heal the Inner Issues That Destroy
Love and Sabotage Your Life

Miracles are Guaranteed
A Step-by-Step Guide to Restoring Love, Being Free,
And Creating A Life That Works

Audio Cassettes

How to Heal a Painful Relationship

Heal the Hurt That Runs Your Life

How to Divorce as Friends

How to Love Yourself

How to Have Love in Your Life

How to be Free of Guilt and Resentment

How to be Free of Upset and Stress

How to Create a Life That Works

How to Create Prosperity

How to Find Your Purpose

How to Experience Your Spirituality

Spirituality: Teachings from a World Beyond

How To Heal A Painful Relationship

AND IF NECESSARY HOW TO PART AS FRIENDS

BILL FERGUSON

Return to the Heart
P.O. Box 541813
Houston, TX 77254

www.billferguson.com
www.divorceasfriends.com

Copyright © 1999 by Bill Ferguson

Return to the Heart
P.O. Box 541813
Houston, Texas 77254
U.S.A.
(713) 520-5370

Cover design by Mark Gelotte

Library of Congress
Catalog Card Number: 98-94052

Second Edition

ISBN 1-878410-25-3

Made in the United States of America

CONTENTS

CONTENTS

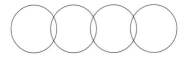

CHAPTER 1

WHAT YOU DO NOW MAKES THE DIFFERENCE

Any relationship can heal. No matter how painful or destructive your relationship may be, it can now be restored. Sound impossible? Well, it's not! Antagonism and defensiveness can be dissolved. Anger and resentment can be replaced with forgiveness and compassion. Conflict can turn into cooperation.

Maybe you'll fall back in love and stay together in a way that works. Maybe you'll need to go your separate ways. Whatever happens, you have the opportunity and ability to heal your relationship. You can be free of the hurt, the anger and the resentment.

The key to healing your relationship is you.

How you interact with the other person determines how that person will interact towards you. How you interact towards each other determines whether your relationship will be painful or supportive.

Once you discover your role in any disharmony, you can heal your relationship. Until this happens, you will forever be ineffective.

As a former divorce attorney, I've worked with many couples whose relationships were painful and destructive. In each instance, the individuals involved were totally unaware of their role in the conflict.

By not being aware of their role in the conflict, there was nothing they could do to end it.

This is what happens in most relationships. We only notice what the other person does to us. We then treat the other person accordingly.

If we receive love and appreciation, we'll give love and appreciation. If we receive criticism and resentment, we'll give criticism and resentment. We call this "giving people what they deserve."

The problem with this is that the other person is doing exactly the same thing. That person only notices what is received from you. Then that person treats you accordingly. Then you treat him or her accordingly.

When you treat each other based on how you get treated, there is no telling what will happen. It's like sailing with no one at the helm. When no one is in charge of the ship, your relationship is in big trouble. You're likely to end up on the rocks.

Usually it's just a matter of time until one of you gets upset. When you get upset, you automatically put up your walls of protection and either resist, attack or withdraw. Then the other person gets upset and does the same thing to you. Then you get more upset and react even more forcefully towards the other.

Without ever knowing, you create a cycle conflict, a cycle of resisting, attacking and withdrawing from each other. This cycle then goes on and on without either person ever noticing his or her role in the problem.

Sides get drawn and issues become something to fight over rather than something to resolve. Walls of protection get fortified and distance grows. The experience of love quickly fades away.

We hurt each other over and over, feeling fully justified for everything we do. Serious damage is done, and none of it is necessary.

If you want to heal your relationship and be free of the suffering, you need to end this cycle of conflict. You need to interact with the other person in a way that works.

Two people are required to create and maintain a cycle of conflict. Only one is needed to end it.

When you put the focus on you and your actions, you can put water on the fire instead of more fuel. You can interact in a way that gains cooperation instead of resentment. You can heal your relationship.

What you do today determines what will happen in your relationship tomorrow. Whether your relationship is painful or supportive is up to you.

EXAMPLE

Helen and Karl constantly argued with each other. Each had become very defensive and critical of the other. They were deep in the cycle of conflict.

When Karl came to my office, he was planning a separation and wanted some advice. Karl knew he had something to do with what was happening, but he didn't know what. All he could see was how Helen treated him.

As we talked, it became obvious that he wanted his relationship to work. He just didn't know how.

The more we visited, the more Karl saw what had happened in his relationship. He saw how much both he and Helen had hurt each other and how each of them had become defensive and resentful towards the other. He saw his role in the cycle of conflict.

I worked with him some more and showed him how to release his anger and resentment. I showed him how to be free of his hurt and restore the love in his relationship.

He was excited with the opportunity and went home to be with Helen.

As Karl applied the principles in this book, he noticed an immediate difference in his relationship.

With his new set of tools and with his anger and resentment gone, Karl was able to interact with Helen in a very different way. He treated her with love.

Helen started feeling safe around Karl. She dropped her defenses and became more understanding and accepting. The arguing stopped.

As time went on, Helen and Karl appreciated each other more and more. They treated each other with love and respect.

By learning how to heal his relationship, Karl was able to end the fighting and restore the love. Now he has a relationship that works, and so can you.

ACTION TO TAKE

◆ Look at your relationship and find the cycle of conflict: the cycle of resisting, attacking and withdrawing from each other.

◆ Notice the pain and frustration that comes from this cycle. Notice how painful this cycle of conflict can be.

◆ Notice that you have something to do with what happens in your relationship. Find your role in the conflict.

◆ Ask yourself these questions: Are you willing to be free of the cycle of conflict? Are you willing to heal your relationship and have it be supportive, whether you live together or apart? Are you willing to learn how?

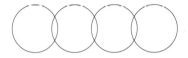

CHAPTER 2

PUT THE FOCUS ON HAVING YOUR RELATIONSHIP WORK

Once you establish an intimate relationship with someone, you will have a relationship with that person for the rest of your life. This is true whether you live together or apart. Even if you move to the North Pole, a part of the other person will still be with you.

To the extent your relationship is supportive, your life will be more enjoyable and more productive. To the extent you have conflict, you will suffer.

You will get upset any time you are with the person or even think about the person. You will become tense and frustrated. You will lose your happiness, your energy and your peace of mind.

When a relationship doesn't work, it affects every aspect of your life. Sometimes the fear and upset can be so consuming that you lose all your effectiveness. You can't move forward.

Even your future relationships are affected. You carry the past wherever you go. Until you heal your relationship, you will never be totally free. The anger and hurt will follow you forever.

The nature of your relationship also determines your ability to resolve issues. Couples who cooperate resolve their issues quickly. Couples who work against each other create a nightmare.

When couples use lawyers and the courthouse to do their fighting, the situation becomes a disaster. Bringing in an adversarial attorney is like bringing in the heavy artillery. Everyone gets hurt. You make your situation much worse.

Whenever you take action to come out on top, without regard to the other person, you create opposition against yourself.

The other person doesn't like coming out second best any more than you do. So whenever you do something to put yourself first and the other person second, you force that person to fight to protect him or herself from you. Then you have to fight to protect yourself from the other person.

You create a cycle of conflict that produces tremendous damage and usually lasts for years. It's just like war.

When you resolve issues by force instead of cooperation, you play tug-of-war with each other's well-being. The name of the game is survival. The motivator is fear and resentment.

When there is no focus on resolving issues, they don't get resolved. Conflict goes on and on with no end in sight. The damage and suffering become greater and greater.

People think that if they just fight hard enough, then somehow the issues will get resolved in their favor. It just doesn't work that way. Issues usually get resolved somewhere in the middle with both sides being disappointed.

People spend a fortune in legal fees and lots of heartache to get what they could have worked out by themselves.

To make matters worse, the divorce decree they've fought over isn't worth much. You can have a decree an inch thick, but it's only as good as the relationship.

When someone is full of anger and resentment, some paper signed by a judge won't gain his or her cooperation. It won't make sure the decree is honored. If someone wants to get back at you, that person will find a way and the decree won't help one bit.

So, as a legal and common sense strategy, it is very important to have your relationship work.

The more you gain the other person's cooperation and concern for your well-being, the easier your life will be. Disagreements get resolved quickly and everyone's well-being will be preserved.

How you interact with the other person will affect the quality of your life from here on out. So put the focus on having your relationship work.

If you decide to go your separate ways, a supportive relationship can allow you to part as friends. If you decide to stay together, a supportive relationship will certainly make your life a lot more enjoyable.

Whatever happens, have your relationship work. Have it work whether you stay together or not.

EXAMPLE

Linda was very judgmental towards Roger. She was constantly putting him down. Then Roger would get upset and put up his walls of protection. Both resented the other and both were deeply hurt.

Finally, Roger moved out. He was so full of anger and resentment, he never wanted to see Linda again.

When Roger came to me, he wanted an attorney who would protect him. As we talked, he soon realized that the best way to protect himself was to make peace with his attacker.

Initially, the thought of making peace with Linda, not only seemed impossible, but counter-productive. He didn't want to have any kind of relationship with her.

Then he realized that he did have a relationship with her, and that this was true whether he liked it or not. The relationship just happened to be a painful one.

Although Roger didn't want to get back together, he knew that his life would be much easier if his relationship with Linda was more constructive. He decided that making peace was worth a try.

He also knew that if his relationship with Linda was going to heal, he would have to initiate the process.

He started by doing whatever he could to make peace. He forgave Linda and accepted her just the way she was. He refused to fight or draw sides against her. He made sure she felt loved, accepted and appreciated.

Gradually, Linda dropped her walls of protection and stopped her fighting. She even became friendly.

As time went on, their relationship became more and more supportive. They enjoyed being with each other and eventually got back together. Now they have a marriage that works.

They could just as easily have gone their separate ways, but if they did, they would have done so as friends.

ACTION TO TAKE

◆ Notice that you will have a relationship with the other person for as long as you live, whether you like it or not. Notice that this is true even if you never see the person again.

◆ Look at the effect this relationship has on the quality of your life. Notice how much easier your life would be if your relationship were supportive.

◆ Notice how much easier the legal process would be if your relationship were supportive.

◆ Do whatever you can to heal your relationship. Make it a top priority. Have your relationship work, whether you stay together or go your separate ways.

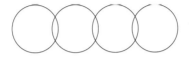

CHAPTER 3

ACKNOWLEDGE THE LOVE THAT'S THERE

We seldom notice the love that's present in painful relationships.

Once two people fall in love, the love is there to stay. You can't push it away even if you wanted to. The excitement and thrill of a relationship may fade but not the love. The love just gets buried by all the upset. We can't see it because of all the anger and hurt.

Love is what makes a difficult relationship so painful. If some stranger rejected you or put you down, you wouldn't be so upset. When the rejection comes from someone you love, it hurts.

People can love each other and still have a lousy relationship. Some people will fight and get on each other's nerves forever. Some people do cruel things to each other. This doesn't mean there's no love.

Now this doesn't make sense. How can you love someone and want a divorce? How can you love someone when you want to have the person shot at sunrise?

We've been taught all these rules about love. When our actions don't match these rules, we invalidate the love that's there.

So don't listen to what you have been taught. Don't look in your head for the love. Look in your heart. Look under the hurt, the anger and the frustration. You will see the love if you want to. The love is there. It is totally separate from your actions and your feelings.

Allow yourself to see how much you still love the other person. Let go of your dreams for how it could have been. Allow the loss. Allow the sadness. Allow the hurt.

As you allow yourself to feel your hurt, the hurt loses power and begins to dissolve. When you fight and resist your hurt, the hurt turns into pain and seems to last forever.

Little children are masters at releasing hurt. This is because they are totally willing to feel their emotions. When they feel hurt, they cry. When they finish crying, their hurt disappears. They bounce right back as though nothing had ever happened.

So be like a child. Be willing to feel your hurt. Cry if you can. It's okay.

Allow yourself to feel your hurt and notice the love that's there.

Once you acknowledge the love, the sting of a painful relationship loses power. The sense of invalidation and rejection fade away. You feel better about yourself and better about your life. You also become far more effective in your relationship.

Once you tell the truth to yourself about how much you love the other person, you can then interact out of the love that's there, rather than out of the anger, the resentment and the hurt.

When you interact with love, you change what happens in your relationship. The other person then begins to feel safe instead of threatened. Walls of protection come down. Often the fighting stops overnight. It's hard to fight with someone who's on your side.

Now this doesn't mean you have to live with the other person or agree with that person's actions. There are times when living together just doesn't work. Some people will get on each other's nerves forever.

It's okay to recognize this and go your separate ways, knowing that under the hurt is the love.

When you operate from the love, your relationship becomes supportive. When you operate from the anger and resentment, you create opposition and resistance. You invite pain and suffering.

There may be times when it seems easier to interact from the anger instead of the love, but it just doesn't work.

When you get angry, look at the truth. You are angry, but you still love the person. It's okay to be angry. It's just not an effective way to relate. Remember:

◆ It's okay to love someone and still want a divorce.

◆ It's okay to love someone and not want to

live with the person.

♦ It's okay to love someone and be hurt.

♦ It's just a matter of telling the truth.

What hurts the most is to love someone and then lie to yourself about it.

EXAMPLE

Mary's relationship with Bob had become so painful that she filed for divorce. She wanted to get as far away from Bob as possible. Then she saw that under all of her anger and frustration, she still loved him.

She didn't notice this before because loving Bob didn't make any sense. How could she love someone and want to leave him? This made no sense, but when she looked, she saw that the love was there.

She loved Bob even though she felt angry and wanted out of the relationship.

Once Mary saw her love for Bob, she realized that Bob probably had the same love for her. The moment she saw this, she started feeling her hurt.

She felt the hurt of losing her relationship and her dreams for how her relationship could have been. She cried and cried. Then, after she finished crying, she felt a wonderful freedom. Most of her hurt and invalidation had disappeared.

Her next concern centered on how to interact with Bob. She wanted to express her love for him, but she was afraid he would take it the wrong way. She didn't want to give him any false hope.

Finally, she decided to take a chance. She told him that she loved him. She loved him, even though she wanted a divorce.

At first, this was hard for Bob to understand, but Mary continued to express her love. Eventually, Bob understood. He then let go of his defensiveness and began to express his love in return.

Mary and Bob still got a divorce, but their relationship became an expression of their love and support for each other. Today they are best friends.

ACTION TO TAKE

◆ Notice that under all the hurt and upset, you still love the other person. You may not want to live with the person, or even see the person; but under the hurt, the love is still there.

◆ Let go of your dreams for how it could have been. Be willing to feel the hurt and the loss. Don't fight the hurt or run from it. Allow it. Cry if you can.

◆ Look beyond the other person's anger and see his or her hurt. Then look beyond that person's hurt and see the love that he or she still has for you.

◆ Interact with the other person out of the love that's there instead of the anger and upset.

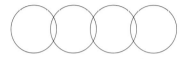

CHAPTER 4

DON'T HANG ON;
LET YOUR PARTNER GO

Relationships don't always work out the way we want. Sometimes relationships become so painful that somebody wants to leave.

If this happens to you, and if you want the other person to stay, how you handle yourself now becomes very important. Usually we push the person further away.

If you want someone to stay, you need to create an environment where the person will want to be with you. So far you haven't done this. If you had, the person wouldn't want to leave.

Now maybe you can turn your relationship around and get back together. It's been done before. Maybe your time together is over and nothing can be done. Maybe it's just too late.

One thing is for sure, you can't force someone to want you. All you can do is treat the person in a way that will have him or her enjoy being with you.

The key to having someone enjoy being with you is to make sure the person feels special. You do this in two ways:

◆ Make sure the person feels loved, accepted and appreciated just the way he or she is.

◆ Give the person his or her freedom. Be willing for the person to be gone tomorrow.

The more you are willing for someone to go, the more you create an environment where he or she can enjoy being with you. This in turn increases the chances of the person wanting to stay.

When you hang on to someone, you do the opposite. You create an environment where the person feels controlled and suffocated. You force the person to fight for breathing room. You push the person away.

Just look at how you feel when someone tries to control you. Hanging on doesn't make someone want to stay. Hanging on makes the person want to leave.

Hanging on also destroys your aliveness and mental well-being. You become consumed by fear and upset. You get tunnel vision and you interact in a way that makes your situation worse.

So, for the sake of your relationship and your sanity, let the person go. Stop hanging on.

To do this, you need to be willing for the person to leave. You don't have to like it or want it to happen. Just be willing.

To the extent you become willing, you release the resistance that creates the fear and the upset. You set yourself free inside and you become far more effective in handling your situation.

By letting go of your demands for how life should be, you can flow with the way life is. You can then see what needs to be done.

Letting someone go is a state of mind and has nothing to do with your actions. It certainly doesn't mean kick the person out. Letting go is what releases the fear and upset so that you can see what action you need to take.

In your heart, be willing for the person to go, but in your actions, do everything you can to create an environment where the other person feels so loved and appreciated that he or she would never want to leave.

To let go, give the person full permission to leave. You can practice this by saying the following words:

"I give you permission to leave, to be gone from my life forever. I don't want you to go, but I want you to be happy. If you have to leave, I understand. You have my love and my blessings whatever you do. I let you go."

If you can say this and mean it, you have set yourself free.

If you have any hesitation, keep saying this over and over. Say it aloud. Imagine the person being in front of you, and give him or her permission to go. Allow yourself to feel the hurt. Cry if you can. Keep saying these words until you can do so without the hurt.

Then get with the other person and say the words directly. This is especially important if you've been hanging on to someone. By giving the person freedom to leave, he or she will feel free of your grasp and will have less reason to avoid you. This makes it easier for the person to stay.

If letting someone go is difficult, look for what you are really avoiding.

People don't leave wonderful, loving relationships. They leave lousy relationships. So why would you hang on to a lousy relationship, especially when hanging on produces so much suffering and is so counter-productive?

We hang on to avoid something inside of ourselves. We don't want to feel the hurt, the loss, or the feelings of being alone or of being abandoned.

We don't want to look at our having failed or of being not good enough. We don't want to be embarrassed or look bad. We don't want to confront our fears of not being able to make it on our own.

We hang on to avoid all the feelings and emotion that would be present if the person were to leave.

What emotions do you get to avoid by hanging on? What feelings and emotion would you have to experience or confront if the person left you? Find what you are really avoiding and see if you are willing to face it.

Notice that you are already feeling this hurt whether you are willing or not.

You don't have a choice whether you are going to feel this hurt. You will. The only choice you have is this: Are you going to allow your hurt like a child and let it go, or are you going to fight the hurt and keep it inside?

As you allow yourself to feel the hurt of losing someone, the hurt loses power, and so does the need to hang on.

To the extent you let go, you become free inside. You restore your aliveness and your peace of mind. You see your situation clearly and you can see what needs to be done.

EXAMPLE

Carla and Paul met and immediately developed an exciting, supportive relationship.

Then Carla started hanging on. She was so afraid of losing Paul that she tried to control his every move. Whenever Paul resisted her control, or whenever she felt threatened, Carla got angry and upset.

Without knowing, she pushed Paul further and further away. Eventually, Paul had enough and moved out.

Carla came to see me searching for a way to save her relationship. She was terrified of losing Paul, and at the same time, she hated him for wanting to leave. She blamed him for everything.

As we talked, Carla began to see the damage she created by hanging on. She still wanted Paul to stay, but she knew that she had to let him go.

Letting him go seemed difficult until she saw what was really going on. As long as she had her relationship, she didn't have to confront her fears of being alone and of being inadequate.

Once she faced her fears and realized that she would be okay no matter what happened, she no longer needed to hang on. When she noticed that Paul was probably gone anyway, letting him go became even easier.

To let Paul go, she imagined herself telling him, "You can go if you want. I won't stand in your way. I love you and I want you to stay, but if you have to go, I understand. I wish you the very best and I want you to be happy. I let you go."

She kept saying this over and over. She felt her hurt and allowed herself to cry. After a few minutes, the tears stopped and she felt an inner peace.

Although she was still afraid, the fear of losing Paul had lost its power. A few days later she saw Paul and gave him his freedom.

She let Paul go. Then every time she saw him, she made sure he felt loved, accepted and appreciated. Before long, Paul realized that it was safe to be around Carla. In fact, he even enjoyed their moments together.

As time went on, Paul spent more and more time with Carla. They started dating and soon created the excitement that was present when they first met. Within a few months Carla and Paul were back in love. Paul moved back in and has enjoyed being with Carla ever since.

Carla saved her relationship when she let Paul go.

ACTION TO TAKE

◆ Be willing for the other person to leave your life forever. You don't have to like it or want it to happen. Just be willing.

◆ If letting someone go is difficult, find what you get to avoid by hanging on. What are the feelings and emotion that you would have to confront? Find what you are really avoiding and be willing to face it.

◆ Imagine the person in front of you and say the words: "I give you full permission to leave, to be gone from my life forever." Say this over and over until you can say it and mean it. Allow yourself to feel the hurt. Cry if you can.

◆ Get with the other person and give him or her the freedom to leave. This is especially important if you have been hanging on.

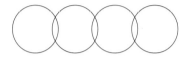

CHAPTER 5

CREATE THE EXPERIENCE OF LOVE

We all want to be loved, accepted and appreciated, just the way we are.

When we feel loved and appreciated by someone, life is wonderful. We feel better about ourselves and better about life. We are happy, alive and free.

This experience of love is what we want in our relationships. When this love is present, relationships are great. When it's absent, relationships are painful.

The presence or absence of love seems to be a function of the other person, but it's not.

The presence or absence of love is a function of how you relate to the other person. In other words, it's a function of you.

You create the experience of love by accepting and appreciating someone just the way the person is.

Look at what happens when someone genuinely accepts and appreciates you, just the way you are. Doesn't this feel great? Of course it does.

You feel better about yourself and everything around you. You also feel better about the person who appreciates you. You then become more accepting and appreciative in return. It's almost impossible not to.

The same thing is true for the other person. Whenever you accept and appreciate someone, with no strings attached, that person feels better about him or herself and better about life. That person also becomes more accepting and appreciative towards you. This happens automatically.

When you give acceptance and appreciation, you receive acceptance and appreciation in return.

The opposite of acceptance and appreciation is non-acceptance, being resentful and critical.

When you give this, you tell the person that he or she is not okay with you. You destroy the experience of love. That person then puts up his or her walls of protection, closes down, and then becomes resentful and critical towards you.

Every interaction you have with another person will either create the experience of love or destroy it, and whatever you give will come right back.

You determine how people treat you by how you treat them. If you want to have love in your life, you have to give love.

If you want your relationship to work, you need to make sure the other person feels loved, accepted and appreciated. Loving someone is never enough. You need to make sure the person feels loved.

So take a look at your relationship. How have you treated the other person? Have you made sure the person feels loved? Have you accepted the person just the way he or she is?

If you look, you will see that you haven't.

Without knowing, you put the other person on the defensive. By your being judgmental and critical, you made him or her judgmental and critical towards you. Then you got upset and became more judgmental and critical in return.

By your non-acceptance, you created the cycle of conflict, the cycle of resisting, attacking and withdrawing from each other.

To heal your relationship, you need to end this cycle of conflict. You need to create the experience of love, not necessarily as husband and wife, but as one human being to another.

Stop criticizing and resisting the other person. Let go of your demands for how you believe he or she should be and make peace with the way he or she is. Stop trying to change the person. Forgive.

The more you create the experience of love in your relationship, the faster you will end the conflict and the faster your relationship will heal.

EXAMPLE

Vicky loved her husband Gary, but their relationship was becoming painful. Both were very defensive and critical of the other. They argued all the time.

Vicky wanted their relationship to be loving and supportive, but she didn't know how.

A friend suggested that she attend one of our programs. Vicky followed her friend's advice and took a good look at how she treated Gary.

She discovered that although she loved Gary, she didn't make sure that Gary felt loved. In fact, she did the opposite. She treated Gary lousy.

Vicky saw how critical and judgmental she had been. She saw how much she had tried to change Gary and how she had damaged the love in their relationship.

She treated Gary according to the way he treated her. If he treated her great, she would treat him great. If he treated her lousy, she would treat him lousy.

Vicky didn't realize it, but she had made

Gary responsible for the presence or absence of love in their relationship.

As soon as she realized this, Vicky decided to treat Gary in a different way.

She treated him with love and respect no matter how he treated her. She made sure he felt loved, accepted and appreciated just the way he was. She stopped trying to change him. She treated him as a friend.

Almost immediately, Gary began treating her differently. He became friendlier and less defensive. As time went on, his walls melted and he became more loving. Now they have a relationship that works.

Vicky turned her relationship around by making sure Gary felt loved, accepted and appreciated.

ACTION TO TAKE

◆ Notice how your actions have damaged the experience of love in your relationship. See how non-accepting, judgmental and critical you have been.

◆ Notice how much you have hurt the other person.

◆ Notice how your actions have forced the other person to protect him or herself from you. Notice how your non-acceptance has fueled the conflict.

◆ To heal your relationship, you need to end the cycle of resisting each other. You need to create the experience of love. Do this by making sure the other person feels loved, accepted and appreciated.

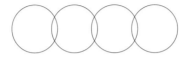

CHAPTER 6

LET THE OTHER PERSON BE THE WAY HE OR SHE IS

The experience of love is created by giving the gift of unconditional acceptance and appreciation. It's letting someone be exactly the way he or she is.

Unfortunately, this is much easier said than done. Some people and the things they do are very difficult to accept. Fortunately, non-acceptance is an illusion.

At any moment, people are the way they are whether you accept them or not. This is also true for the other person in your relationship. No matter how difficult that person may be, that person is still the way he or she is.

How you feel about the person is totally irrelevant. Hating the way someone is doesn't change a thing. That person is still the way he or she is.

Acceptance is nothing more than being at peace with the truth.

When you are at peace with the truth of how someone is, you can see what you need to do, and you can interact in a way that is supportive.

When you fight the way someone is, you create a state of upset. You lose your ability to see clearly, and you interact in a way that creates opposition and resistance against yourself.

We think that if we just get upset enough, the other person will somehow get the hint and become exactly the way we want him or her to be. Obviously, this doesn't happen.

In fact, the more you resist the way someone is, the worse that person becomes.

Look at how you feel when someone resists or tries to change you. How do you feel about changing? You don't want to. You get upset and resistant. You could care less about changing.

You also become more judgmental and critical toward the person.

The same thing happens when you resist someone else. That person then gets hurt and puts up his or her walls of protection. Then automatically, that person either resists, attacks or withdraws. That person acts just like you do when someone resists or tries to change you.

When you can't be at peace with the truth of how someone is, you destroy love and make your situation worse. You fuel the cycle of conflict. As this cycle grows, the experience of love disappears. The relationship suffers and everyone gets hurt.

Life becomes one big upset, and the other person seems to be the cause. But this isn't the truth. The other person is just the way he or she is. The cause of the upset is you. You create the upset by not allowing the other person to be the way he or she is.

Resisting the truth is like demanding that the zebra grow spots or that the sun doesn't set. Resisting the truth doesn't change a thing. It just creates more suffering.

When you give up your demands for how

someone should be and make peace with the way he or she is, you release your upset. You restore your ability to see what needs to be done.

Letting someone be the way he or she is, is an act of granting permission, a declaration of allowing. It's saying, "I give you full permission to be the way you are, and I give up my right to complain about it forever."

This doesn't mean that you like the way the person is or approve of what he or she does. It just means that you are at peace with the truth.

Once you let the other person be the way he or she is, you may discover that he or she isn't the type of person you want to live with. That's okay. You don't have to live with the person.

You can let the person be exactly the way he or she is, somewhere else. You don't have to hold your breath waiting for a miracle. You can let the person be the way he or she is, and you can get on with your life.

You also don't have to give the person whatever he or she demands. You don't have to let the person do whatever he or she feels like doing. Sometimes you need to say no.

Sometimes you need to take a strong stand to keep from being bowled over.

Do whatever you need to do to have your life work. Just make sure the person feels loved, accepted and appreciated in the process.

When you resist someone, you create resistance against yourself, and it's uphill all the way. When you can accept and appreciate someone, you create an environment of cooperation and support.

So let go of your demands for how the person should be and let the person be the way he or she is. Then do whatever you need to do.

EXAMPLE

Marci had a habit of not keeping her word, and Randy hated it. He did everything he could to get her to change this, but nothing worked. She kept breaking her promises and Randy kept getting upset.

Finally, he realized that Marci was the way that she was and would probably never keep her word. He didn't like this, but he realized that he couldn't change her.

Randy then had a choice. He could either continue getting upset, which by now was clearly damaging their relationship, or he could stop trying to change Marci and accept her the way that she was.

To accept her, he had to be willing for her never to keep her word with him. He had to let go of his expectations for how she should be and make peace with the way that she was.

He decided to meet with Marci and actually give her permission to never keep her word. He hated doing this, but he knew that this was something he had to do. Besides, Marci would do what she wanted whether Randy gave her permission or not.

So he gritted his teeth and gave her the permission. He said, "Marci, you don't ever have to keep your word with me again. I hope you do, but if you don't, I won't complain."

Randy then handled his affairs so that he didn't have to depend on Marci.

Within a few days, Randy noticed that he no longer got upset when Marci didn't keep her word. When she did keep her word, it was a pleasant surprise.

By Randy's letting go of his demands and expectations for how Marci should be, his upset went away and his relationship began to heal. Ironically, Marci started to keep her word.

ACTION TO TAKE

◆ Notice that the other person is exactly the way he or she is whether you like it or not. Notice how irrelevant your feelings are.

◆ Notice how much you have fought and resisted the way that person is. Notice the conflict you have created by your resistance.

◆ Let go of your demands for how that person should be and make peace with the way the person is. Give him or her full permission to be that way forever.

◆ Remember that acceptance is nothing more than surrendering to the truth. You don't have to like the way the person is and you don't have to live with the person. You just need to make peace with the truth.

◆ Give all the people in your life full permission to be the way they are. Work with this until you can.

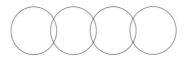

CHAPTER 7

HEAL YOUR HURT

When you were born, you were created with the natural ability to heal hurt. Look at little children. Little children are masters at healing hurt.

When a child feels hurt, the child cries. Then, after the child finishes crying, the hurt is all gone.

Little children are able to release their hurt because they do something that we don't notice. They allow their hurt. They are totally willing to feel all their feelings and emotions.

This is the natural process for healing

hurt. Hurt is just a feeling. When you allow the feeling to take its course, the feeling quickly comes and goes.

Unfortunately, we have been taught to do the opposite. Instead of allowing our hurt, we have been taught to fight it. "Big boys and girls don't cry. If you want something to cry about, I'll give you something to cry about."

You soon learn to avoid your hurt. This then circumvents the natural healing process. Instead of allowing the feelings and letting them go, you fight the feelings and keep them inside.

You try to push the hurt away, but you can't. The hurt isn't outside of you, it's inside. So, in your attempt to push the hurt away, you actually push the hurt deeper inside. You then spend the rest of your life running from this suppressed hurt.

No matter what you do to avoid this hurt, you'll never get away from it. You'll keep feeling this hurt whether you like it or not.

When you're hurt, you're hurt. You don't have a choice whether you are going to feel it. You will. Your only choice is this: Are you going to allow your hurt like a child and let it go, or are you going to fight your hurt and keep it inside?

If you allow the hurt, the feelings disappear. If you fight the hurt, the feelings turn into pain and then stay.

To see this in your life, find a time when you were hurt and you allowed yourself to cry. Then, after you cried your last tear, you felt a wonderful freedom. This was a time when you allowed your hurt.

Now find a time when you were hurt and hated it. You hated your circumstances and you hated your hurt. Notice that this hurt was very painful and seemed to stay forever.

The key to releasing your hurt is to be willing to experience it. Keep telling yourself, "It's okay to feel the hurt. It's okay." Let the hurt come and let the hurt go. Cry if you can.

Crying is the most powerful tool for releasing hurt.

If the hurt is there but you don't feel any tears, fake it. Fake the crying until you get into the emotion. Then experience all the hurt as deeply as you can.

You may notice certain thoughts as you cry: "Why did she do this?" "Why can't she love me?" Let the thoughts guide your crying. Cry each thought. Then move to the next one.

Reach in and grab all the hurt you can. Experience it fully. Then, when the hurt is fully experienced, it goes away.

If you are in a painful relationship, you will probably experience waves of hurt. Use each wave for all the healing you can get.

If the hurt doesn't release, there is something that you are resisting. You are probably fighting the feelings of being not good enough, not worth loving, a failure, or some other form of being not okay.

EXAMPLE

Carrie and Robert lived together for several years before they broke up. They loved each other. They just didn't live well together.

When they broke up, Robert had lots of sadness. Occasionally he would shed some tears, but mostly, he kept his hurt inside. Even when he did shed tears, he would fight his hurt.

He was taught that men shouldn't cry. Men should be strong and keep their emotions inside. The problem with this was that Robert was hurt and he couldn't release the emotion.

Robert was so full of hurt that it consumed him. He kept thinking about his lost relationship and what went wrong. He couldn't get on with his life.

When Robert and I met, he realized that he had been suppressing his hurt. He then went home to heal as much of his hurt as he could.

He tried to cry, but it was difficult. So he got some old photographs of Carrie and turned on some of their special music. The hurt became much stronger, but he still couldn't cry.

Then he tried faking the tears. Before long, the tears started flowing. Soon, he was crying uncontrollably. He felt the hurt of losing Carrie and the hurt of feeling not worth loving. He cried as hard as he could.

The hurt seemed like it would never go away, but after about forty minutes, the hurt suddenly lifted. Robert then felt a joy and peace that he hadn't had in months.

A few days later, Robert had another wave of hurt. He welcomed the hurt because it was another opportunity for healing. He cried and cried. After about thirty minutes the hurt went away.

Robert had a total of three waves of hurt. Each time, he used the opportunity to release as much of his hurt as possible. After the third wave, most of his hurt was gone.

After that, Robert felt sadness from time to time, but he had learned how to cry and release his hurt.

By allowing his hurt and shedding his tears, Robert was able to release the emotion that had created so much pain.

ACTION TO TAKE

◆ Be willing to feel your hurt and the feelings of being not okay. Keep telling yourself, "It's okay to feel the hurt. It's okay." Let the hurt come and let the hurt go.

◆ Notice that you don't have a choice about whether you are going to feel your hurt. You will. Your only choice is to allow the hurt and let it go, or fight the hurt and keep it inside.

◆ Use every opportunity to release more hurt. Whenever you feel hurt, cry. If you don't feel any tears, fake the tears until they become real. Release as much of the hurt as you can.

◆ Notice the freedom and inner peace that you experience after you release the hurt. Notice how painful it is when you fight the hurt.

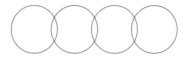

CHAPTER 8

FIND THE INNER ISSUES THAT DESTROY LOVE

When we get upset, we think that the upset is caused by what happens, but this is an illusion that will keep you stuck forever. Upsets are never caused by what happens. Upsets are caused by fighting and resisting what happens.

To see this in your life, select a recent upset. Now notice what would happen to the upset if somehow you were at peace with what happened. There would be no upset.

There would be no upset because the upset wasn't caused by what happened. The upset was caused by your fighting and resisting what happened. If you could take away the fighting and resisting, there would be no upset.

We fight what happens because we don't want to feel all the hurt that gets reactivated by what happens. In other words, our circumstances have just struck a nerve.

This is why the same thing can happen to two people and one person will get upset and the other won't. Different people get upset at different things because each person has a different set of suppressed hurt.

You may never notice this hurt, but it is certainly there. It determines your actions and shapes your life.

A good way to see this hurt is to notice what happens the moment you get upset. Notice the immediate surge of feelings and emotion that come forth. This is the hurt that runs your life.

Any circumstance that may reactivate this hurt then becomes a serious threat that must be avoided at all cost. To protect yourself from this threat, you automatically fight, resist and hang on.

This resisting is what sabotages both your

relationship and your life. It destroys love and creates all your fear and upset. It fuels the cycle of conflict and is responsible for all your unworkability, all your suffering and all your self-sabotaging behavior.

So, to be most effective in your relationship and in your life, you need to find and heal this hurt.

To start the healing process, let's look at how these issues get created.

When you were born, you were pure love. But you were born into a world that suppresses love. So, in the process of growing up, you got hurt. You experienced very painful losses of love.

As a little child, the only way you could explain these painful losses of love was to blame yourself. In a moment of hurt, you bought the notion that you were worthless, not good enough, a failure, not worth loving, or in some other way, not okay.

This wasn't the truth, but to a little child, this was the only explanation that made any sense at the time.

You then hated the very notion that you

created. "No one can ever love me if I'm worth-less. Worthless is a horrible way to be."

From that moment on, the underlying focus of your life would be to avoid this hurt.

The irony is that the more you fight these feelings of being not okay, the stronger they become and the more they run your life. Avoiding these feelings is what gives them power.

Here is a short exercise that demonstrates this:

Imagine four large yellow balloons on the ceiling above you, but don't think about them. Whatever you do, don't think about those four large yellow balloons on the ceiling above you. You just thought about them. Don't do that.

Notice what happens when you try not to think about the balloons. You keep thinking about them. In fact, you can hardly think about anything else. By resisting the thought of the yellow balloons, you keep the thought alive.

The same is true with the feelings of being worthless, not good enough, or whatever your issue is. Ultimately, these feelings are only thoughts, but by your resisting these thoughts, you give them power and carry them with you day after day.

To heal this hurt and to set yourself free inside, you need to do the opposite of fighting and resisting. You need to find the specific hurt that you've been avoiding and make peace with it. As you do this, the hurt loses power and goes away.

The best way to find your hurt is to look at your upsets.

Make a list of all the major upsets that you have had in your life. Then look at the hurt that's under each upset and ask yourself this question: "What do those circumstances say about me?"

If someone is leaving you, this could say that you're not worth loving. If you lost your job, this could say that you are a failure. For each upset, find what those circumstances say about you.

Then notice that the same hurt keeps showing up in your life. This is the hurt that runs your life.

Find the words that most accurately describe this hurt. Find the words that hurt the most. This hurt will always be some form of "not okay."

Once you find this hurt, you won't like it. You may even want to deny it, but whether you like it or not, that hurt is there, and it runs your life.

After you find the specific hurt that you've been running from, the next step is to do the opposite of fighting it, which is to embrace it.

The best way to do this is to look in your life and see that this is indeed, an aspect of you. It has to be. It wouldn't keep popping up in your life if it wasn't there.

So look in your life and see all the evidence to prove that you are not good enough, not worth loving or whatever else you may be resisting. The evidence is there if you are willing to see it. You don't have to like it. You just have to tell the truth about it.

Worthless is part of you. It's also no big deal. You are also worthy. Worthy and worthless are both aspects of being human.

So allow yourself to be human. Allow yourself to feel all the hurt of being worthless, not good enough, not worth loving or whatever your issue is.

As you own this part of you, and as you allow yourself to feel the hurt of being this way, both the aspect and the hurt lose their power.

Then something very special happens.

You no longer need to avoid the hurt of worthless and you no longer need to be worthy. You can just be you.

This is a wonderful freedom!

The moment this happens, you become more at peace with yourself and more able to flow with life.

You also become far more effective in your relationship.

Keep working with this until you can say, "Yes, I'm worthless. So what! I'm also worthy."

If you want to learn more about how to find and heal this hurt, read the book, *Heal The Hurt That Runs Your Life*, or listen to the book on tape. The healing process is also covered in detail in the audio cassettes, *How To Divorce As Friends*.

If you want to heal your hurt quickly, have a telephone consulting session with Bill Ferguson or a member of his staff. The phone number is 713-520-5370.

EXAMPLE

When Rhonda was growing up, her father was so preoccupied with his work that he seldom paid any attention to her. When he did pay attention, he would yell at her. She felt totally unloved.

As a result, Rhonda couldn't help but buy the notion that she wasn't worth loving. This wasn't the truth, but this became a hurt that she would spend the rest of her life running from.

To avoid this hurt, Rhonda interacted in a way that sabotaged all of her relationships.

Anytime something implied that she wasn't worth loving, she would become full of fear and upset. She would try to control life and force people to be a certain way.

No matter how hard the men in her life tried, they could never treat Rhonda "worth loving" enough. She would constantly be upset about one thing or another.

She would also hang on to the men in her life. She had to, because if someone left, that would prove that she was not worth loving. To avoid this hurt she hung on.

Rhonda was so hard to live with, she pushed everyone away.

Finally, after her third and most painful divorce, she noticed that there was a pattern in her life. She realized that she must have something to do with her relationship problems.

This was the point when Rhonda's life turned around.

It wasn't hard for Rhonda to see that "not worth loving" was an aspect of her. She spent her entire life running from this, but now the hurt was so much in her face, she could no longer deny it. The evidence was overwhelming.

As she owned this aspect of herself and allowed herself to cry, the hurt that ran her life began to dissolve. She then realized that "not worth loving" was just part of being human. What a wonderful freedom.

"I'm not worth loving. How great! Now I don't have to prove to myself and to everyone else that I am worth loving. Now I can just be me." She started laughing once she saw the joke that she had been playing on herself.

From that moment on, the hurt had lost

its power.

Rhonda was then able to go on and find the relationship of her dreams, and most importantly, she was able to keep it.

ACTION TO TAKE

◆ Make a list of the times in your life when you've been upset.

◆ Then look at the hurt that's under each upset and find what that hurt is. What do those circumstances say about you? Do they say that you are not good enough, not worth loving or a failure? Find the words that hurt the most.

◆ Look in your life and find all the evidence to prove that this is an aspect of you. This is not the only aspect of you. It's only one of many, but this one is certainly there. It wouldn't keep popping up in your life if it wasn't there.

◆ Allow yourself to feel the hurt of being this way. Let in this aspect of you. Cry if you can. To the extent that you are able to own this part of you, the hurt loses power and disappears.

◆ Remember that being not okay is just a notion that you created in a moment of hurt. It isn't the truth. It just feels that way.

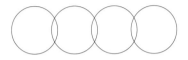

CHAPTER 9

FORGIVE; LET GO OF YOUR RESENTMENTS

Nothing destroys the experience of love faster and more powerfully than a resentment.

When you resent someone you are saying, "I strongly dislike you," which is the exact opposite of accepting and appreciating someone.

Resentments create very painful relationships. When you resent someone, you forcefully destroy the experience of love. The other person then gets upset and gives it right back to you. Then you become even more resentful.

You quickly create the cycle of resisting,

attacking and withdrawing from each other. It's impossible to establish or maintain a good relationship with someone you resent.

Resentments also produce a great deal of internal suffering. When you are full of resentment, you can't move forward. Your aliveness, your peace of mind, and your clarity all go out the window.

Resentments act like poison. They eat at you. They keep you upset and they keep you from enjoying your life. When you have a resentment, a major part of you closes down. If you have lots of resentment, you will have lots of suffering and very little love.

Resentments are like thorns in your side. You need to pull all of them out one at a time. Until you do, you will never be free.

Ironically, the only one who really suffers when you resent is you. The other person is out enjoying his or her life while you stay stuck in your upset. You have to pay the price, not only for what the other person did, but for your resentment as well.

Usually, the suffering that's caused by your resentment is much worse than anything the other person may have done.

Resentments seem to be caused by the other person, but they're not. The other person just did what he or she did, and you resented it. No one has the power to create a resentment in you. Only you can do that.

That's why the same thing can happen to two different people, and one person will have a resentment and the other won't. Resentments are not caused by what happened. They are caused by how we handle what happened.

When we resent someone, we are saying very forcefully that the other person is the cause, the problem, and the fault. Not us!

We resent in a subconscious attempt to keep the spotlight on the other person. We point at the other person so we don't have to look at ourselves.

If we were to look at ourselves, we would have to experience all the hurt of feeling not good enough, not worth loving, a failure, or whatever our issue is. We would have to confront our responsibility for what happened and our responsibility for what we now need to do.

To avoid this hurt, we blame. This in turn creates a state of upset that destroys love and fuels the cycle of conflict.

So, to restore both your peace of mind and your effectiveness, you need to let go of your resentment.

The first step in releasing a resentment is to see if you are willing to let it go.

Look and see if your resentment forwards you in life. Have you suffered enough? Are you now willing to let it go?

You might as well. Besides, letting go of resentment isn't for the benefit of the other person. It's for the benefit of you.

The second step in releasing a resentment is to find and heal the hurt that you're avoiding.

To find the hurt that's under your resentment, ask yourself: "What do those circumstances say about me?" Do they say that I'm not good enough, not worth loving, a failure or some other form of not okay?

Find the words that hurt the most and be willing to feel the hurt of being that way. Look in your life and see all the evidence to prove that this is indeed an aspect of you. Cry if you can.

Remember, you don't have any choice about whether you are going to feel this hurt. You will. The only choice you have is to either allow the hurt like a child, and let it go, or fight the hurt and keep it inside.

So be willing. Be willing to feel all the hurt from what happened. As you allow yourself to feel this hurt, you lose your need for the resentment.

The next step in releasing a resentment is to notice that the other person is doing the very best that he or she can with his or her very limited equipment.

If you look, at any moment, every one of us has a very particular state of mind and a very particular way of viewing life. This limited view of life is based on the avoidance of fear and hurt. It's created by all our experiences and all the decisions that we've made about life.

This self-created reality then shapes the way we live our lives.

Often our past is so full of fear and hurt that the reality we create is very destructive.

Sometimes we do lots of damage, but if you

look, we are always doing the very best we can with the very limited skills and awareness that we have at the moment.

In every situation, we do what we think we should, based on how we see life at the time. Sometimes we see life very narrowly. Sometimes we make big mistakes.

Notice that the person you resent acts totally consistent with the way he or she views life.

If the person was wiser and more aware, then he or she could have handled things very differently, but the person isn't wiser and more aware. That person only knows what he or she knows.

So here's the big question, "Are you willing to forgive the person for not being wiser and more aware?" You might as well.

Use the following questions to let go of your resentment.

◆ Are you willing to be free of your resentment?

◆ Are you willing to feel all the hurt of being not good enough, not worth loving, a failure, or whatever your issue is?

◆ Can you look in your life and see all the evidence to prove that these are aspects of you?

◆ Are you willing to feel all the hurt from what happened?

◆ Doesn't the person you resent have a very particular state of mind and a very particular way of seeing life?

◆ Doesn't this person act totally consistent with his or her limited reality?

◆ Do you see how much this person suffers as a result of his or her limited reality?

◆ If the person was wiser and more aware, wouldn't the person be able to interact quite differently?

◆ Do you see that the person isn't wiser and more aware, that this person only knows what he or she knows?

◆ Are you willing to forgive the person for not knowing, for not being wiser and more aware?

◆ Doesn't this person do the very best that he or she can with his or her very limited ability?

◆ Are you willing to forgive the person for acting consistent with his or her limited ability?

◆ Are you willing to forgive the person for all the damage that was done as a result of his or her limited ability?

◆ Are you willing to forgive the person for everything?

◆ Do you now let go of all resentment for the person, just because you say so?

If you say no to any of these questions, that's where you are stuck. Keep working with each question until you can say yes, and mean it.

If you have any resentment left, see if you can release it by your declaration. "I now release all resentment for the person. I release it just because I say so."

If you still have a resentment, look at what you get to avoid by hanging on to it. What would you have to experience or be responsible for if you lost your resentment? Are you willing to experience the hurt, the loss and the feelings of being not okay?

Are you willing to take responsibility for what happened? Are you willing to be responsible for what you now have to do? Look for what you are avoiding and see if you are willing to face it.

Sometimes a resentment can be released in an instant. That's how long you took to put it there. Sometimes, it may take longer. Sometimes you need to keep forgiving the person over and over until the resentment disappears.

Keep working with this until you are totally free of all resentment.

EXAMPLE

Barbara's husband Michael had an affair, and she resented him for it. She wanted to stay together and forget what had happened, but she couldn't. Every time she saw Michael, she got upset.

Barbara so resented Michael and what happened, she could no longer be effective in her relationship. She put up her walls and wouldn't allow herself to be open and loving. She became angry and critical. Her relationship grew worse every day.

She knew she had to forgive Michael, but she didn't know how.

When we met, I asked her to look at what was behind her resentment. What was the hurt that she was avoiding? What did the resentment protect her from?

When Barbara looked, she discovered her fear. She didn't want to confront the possibility that Michael had an affair because she wasn't good enough. Just the thought of being not good enough brought up lots of old hurt.

Then she looked in her life and saw that

not good enough was indeed an aspect of her. She hated this, but she saw that this was true. She faced her hurt and cried.

When she finished crying, she felt an deep, inner freedom. Most of the hurt and the feelings of being not good enough were gone.

Without realizing it, Barbara created her resentment so she wouldn't have to deal with her hurt. Once she was willing to face this hurt, she no longer needed the resentment. She could then forgive.

As soon as she let go of her resentment, she fell back in love with Michael. Her anger and defensiveness had disappeared.

Barbara and Michael restored the love in their relationship, and since then, Michael has never felt the need to be with another woman.

Barbara healed her relationship the moment she let go of her resentment.

ACTION TO TAKE

◆ Notice how much you have suffered as a result of your resentment. Notice what it has done to your peace of mind and to your relationship. Have you suffered enough? Are you now willing to let it go?

◆ Find the hurt that is under your resentment. What do those circumstances say about you? Find the words that hurt the most.

◆ Be willing to feel all the hurt from what happened. Be willing to feel the hurt of feeling worthless, not good enough, not worth loving or whatever your issue is.

◆ Use the questions in this chapter to release your resentment for the other person. Work with this until all your resentment is gone.

◆ Do the same for every person in your life. Set yourself free of all resentment.

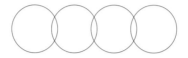

CHAPTER 10

ACCEPT YOUR 100% RESPONSIBILITY

At any moment, you are totally at the effect of everything around you. Whatever happens, you will react in some way. You may get angry or bored. You may do one thing or another, but you will always react. You are 100% at the effect of life.

At the same time, everything around you is totally at the effect of you. Whatever you do, your environment will in some way react to you. That makes you the cause.

You are 100% the cause of everything around you. At the same time, you are 100% at the effect. You react to the world around you, and at the same time, the world around you reacts to you.

This is also true in relationships. Each person is totally at the effect of the other. At the same time, each person is cause.

If someone gets mad and yells at you, obviously that person is the cause of your upset. At the same time, you did something that resulted in the person getting angry. You also determine how you react to the anger. That makes you cause. Whether the anger was fair or not is irrelevant. You are still both cause and effect.

If someone has an affair, that person is clearly responsible. So is his or her spouse. People usually have affairs to find love and appreciation. If this was sufficiently provided at home, there wouldn't have been an affair. Both are totally responsible.

Relationships are not 50/50. They are 100/100.

How you treat someone determines how that person will treat you. If you treat someone with love, acceptance and appreciation, that person will react one way. If you are judgmental and critical toward someone, that person will react in a very different way.

Like it or not, you are fully responsible for what happens in your relationship.

Fortunately, the other side of the coin is also true. The other person is also fully responsible. How that person treats you determines how you will react. If the person is loving, accepting and appreciative of you, you will react one way. If the person is judgmental and critical, you will react another way.

Both of you are totally, 100% responsible for the presence or absence of love.

Now this is not what we have been taught. We've been taught that there is only one responsibility. Either it's over there with the other person, it's with you, or it somehow gets divided 50/50.

When we look at our situation, we quickly determine where the responsibility lies. It's over there with the other person. That person is clearly the problem.

Everything you say about the other person is the truth. That person really is 100% responsible.

The trouble with this is that even though

you are telling the truth, you are only seeing one side of the coin. You are also responsible.

When you blame someone, you give that person all your power. You put that person at cause and you put yourself at effect. In other words, you make yourself a victim.

When all the responsibility is with the other person, there is nothing you can do about your situation. You become powerless.

So, to get your power back, you have to see your full responsibility for the mess. You don't have to like it, just see it.

When you can see your role in the problem, you can do something about it. You can turn your situation around.

Once you discover that you single-handedly destroyed the love in your relationship, both you and your relationship are on the way to some very major healing. As long as you point at the other person, you will stay stuck forever.

So take a look. Notice how you treated the other person. Find your 100% responsibility for the loss of love. The other person is also fully responsible, but look at yourself first.

◆ You didn't accept the person exactly the way he or she was.

◆ You didn't make sure the other person felt loved, accepted and appreciated.

◆ You fought and resisted the person.

◆ You created the conflict in your relationship.

◆ You single-handedly destroyed the love and pushed the person away.

If you look, you will see that all of these statements are true. If they weren't, you wouldn't have a painful relationship.

You can also say the same thing about the other person, and it will be true. Blaming just doesn't change anything. Blaming only makes your situation worse. So stop looking at the other person and look at yourself.

As you let in your responsibility, you may experience some sadness and loss. That's okay. This can be very healing. Just allow the hurt, and let it go.

If you notice that you are blaming yourself, don't. Blame and responsibility are two different things. Responsibility is telling the truth. Blame and fault are judgments that get added. If you are hanging on to any blame or fault, let it go. Forgive yourself.

You may have made some big mistakes. So have the rest of us. Remember, you did the very best you could with the limited awareness that you had at the time.

◆ Forgive yourself for not being wiser and more aware.

◆ Forgive yourself for doing what you thought you should.

◆ Forgive yourself for any damage that you may have caused.

◆ Let go of the past and get on with your life.

Once you let in your 100% responsibility for the loss of love in your relationship, you can no longer blame the other person. You automatically become more accepting and more effective.

You can then interact in a way that creates love instead of more conflict.

EXAMPLE

Ed and Joanne were deep in the cycle of conflict for most of their marriage. After about seven years of suffering, Ed had enough and filed for divorce. Then the conflict spread to the courthouse. They spent a fortune in attorney fees.

Eventually their divorce was over, but the conflict continued. They fought over visitation and the discipline of their two children.

After nine years of conflict, Ed wanted some relief. He came to one of our workshops and had two realizations that changed his life.

First, he discovered that under his hatred for Joanne, there was a tremendous amount of hurt. Then, under the hurt, he saw that he still loved her. He didn't want to live with her or even see her, but he couldn't deny that the love was there.

Then he had his second and most important realization. He realized that he had single-handedly destroyed the love in his relationship. All the painful things that Joanne did to him were a direct result of the painful things that he had done to her.

Up to that point, Ed could never see his role in the conflict. He could only see how Joanne had treated him. Now he saw his role very clearly.

He saw how judgmental and critical he had been. He saw how much he had hurt Joanne and how he had forced her to protect herself from him. He saw his 100 % responsibility for the loss of love in their relationship.

He didn't like what he saw, but he couldn't deny it.

The next time he saw Joanne, he took responsibility for all their suffering. He asked her to forgive him. He then did everything he could to make sure she felt loved, accepted and appreciated.

The relationship changed almost over night. For the first time in years, Joanne felt safe around Ed. She let go of her protectiveness and stopped fighting him. Both of them became more accepting of the other.

They never got back together, and they continued to keep their distance, but the constant conflict of the past had disappeared.

ACTION TO TAKE

◆ Notice how you have single-handedly destroyed the love in your relationship. See how judgmental and critical you've been. Work with this until you can clearly see your 100% responsibility.

◆ Notice how much you have hurt the other person and pushed the person away. Notice that everything the other person has done to you has been a direct result of what you've done to him or her.

◆ Notice that by blaming the other person, you have lost your power and made yourself a victim. Notice how your blaming has fueled the conflict.

◆ Refuse to blame the other person for anything. That person is also 100% responsible, but blaming doesn't change a thing. Keep looking for your 100%.

◆ Forgive yourself for all the mistakes that you've made.

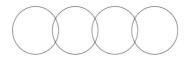

CHAPTER 11

FORGIVE YOURSELF

The key to releasing guilt is to recognize that we all go through life doing the very best we can with the very limited skills and awareness that we have at the time.

Unfortunately, the awareness that we have is seldom enough. As a result, we make mistakes. Sometimes we make big ones.

Making mistakes is just part of the human process. That's how we learn. Every time you make a mistake, you learn a little more about life. You become a little wiser and a little more aware.

If you look, the most valuable lessons you

have ever learned are lessons that you could only have learned the hard way.

It's too bad that we have to learn so much by making mistakes. The real tragedy happens when we add guilt.

The moment you add guilt, you seriously damage your relationship with yourself. You lose your confidence and your self-respect. You reinforce the feelings of being not okay. You feel undeserving and you hold yourself back.

Guilt seems to be caused by what you did, but it's not. Guilt is never caused by what you did. Guilt is something that you add later with the benefit of hindsight.

It was only after you discovered the consequences of your actions did you add guilt.

At the moment you made your mistake, you were doing exactly what you thought you should, given the state of mind you had at the time. Only with hindsight could you have acted differently.

Even if you thought you knew better, your level of knowing wasn't enough to change your actions. You certainly didn't know the consequences like you do today.

"But I should have known." Nonsense. You couldn't possibly have known one moment before you did. Making the mistake is how you learned.

Five years from now you are going to be much wiser than you are today, but the wisdom that you're going to have in five years doesn't do you any good today. That's because today, you don't have it. You only know what you know.

Likewise, the wisdom that you have today didn't do you any good back then. Back then, you only knew what you knew.

So here's the big question: "Are you willing to forgive yourself for not knowing? Are you willing to forgive yourself for not being wiser and more aware?" You might as well.

If you look, you did the very best you could, given where you were at the time.

Maybe now you have suffered enough. Ask yourself, "Are you willing to be free of your guilt? Have you punished yourself enough?" See if you are willing to set yourself free.

If you are, find a specific incident that you feel guilty about.

Then go back in time to the moment that you did whatever you did. Put yourself back in the state of mind that you had at the time.

Then ask yourself these questions:

◆ At that moment, didn't you see life in a very particular way? Didn't you have a very particular state of mind?

◆ Didn't you act totally consistent with that state of mind and with the way you saw life at that moment?

◆ If you knew then what you know today, if you had a different state of mind, wouldn't you have been able to interact very differently?

◆ You didn't know then what you know today, did you? You only knew what you knew, and that wasn't enough.

◆ Didn't you do the very best you could with the limited skills and awareness that you had at the time?

◆ Are you willing to feel the hurt from what you did?

◆ Are you willing to forgive yourself for not knowing and for not being wiser and more aware?

◆ Are you willing to forgive yourself for acting consistent with your limited awareness?

◆ Are you willing to forgive yourself for the damage that you caused as a result of what you did?

◆ Do you now totally forgive yourself for not being wiser and more aware, and for doing what you did? Do you now let go of all guilt just because you say so?

◆ Are you willing to forgive yourself for everything that you have ever done?

Ultimately, forgiveness is just a choice. "I forgive myself. I'm sad and I regret what happened, but I forgive myself. I forgive myself just because I say so."

If releasing a guilt seems to be particularly difficult, you are probably resisting the hurt of being worthless, not good enough or some other form of not okay. Find what your actions say about you. Then allow yourself to feel the hurt of being this way. Allow yourself to be human.

Do whatever it takes to be free of all your guilt. Forgive yourself for everything you have ever done. Remember that you have always done the very best you could with the limited skills and awareness that you had at the time.

EXAMPLE

David and Susan had a good relationship until David started playing around with other women. Susan hoped that David would get this running around out of his system, but he didn't. Susan stayed as long as she could, but eventually she couldn't stand the hurt any more and left.

Not until Susan was gone did David realize how much he loved her. He tried desperately to get her back, but he was too late. She had been hurt too many times and didn't want to take another chance.

David threw away a good relationship and hurt a wonderful person in the process. He hated himself for what he had done.

Four years later his guilt still plagued him, robbing him of his aliveness and keeping him from loving himself. This guilt held him back in his relationships and in his life.

David talked about his guilt in one of our workshops. He said it wouldn't go away.

I then asked him if he was willing to be forgiven. Was he willing to be free of his guilt? To his surprise, he noticed a hesitancy. Part of him wanted to keep the guilt. Part of him didn't want to be free.

Then I had him look at how much he had suffered from his guilt. I asked him if he had been punished enough. He said that he had and that he was now ready to be free.

I worked with David until he could see that he did the best he could with limited awareness that he had at the time.

I asked him if he would have acted very differently if he knew then what he knows today. The answer was yes, of course. He would have acted very differently, but he didn't know.

Then I asked David if he was willing to forgive himself for not knowing, for not being wiser and more aware than he was.

Once David realized that he did the best he could with his limited awareness, he was able to forgive himself. Instantly David felt different inside. He felt free and alive. The burden was gone.

David had no idea how much he had suffered until he forgave himself and set himself free.

ACTION TO TAKE

◆ Notice how much you have suffered as a result of your guilt. Notice how your guilt has robbed you of your confidence, your happiness and your self-respect.

◆ See if you are willing to be free of your guilt.

◆ Make a list of everything you have ever done that you feel guilty about. Then use the questions in this chapter to release each item of guilt.

◆ Remember that you have always done the very best you could with the limited skills and awareness that you have had at the time. If you were wiser and more aware, you could have handled your situation very differently, but you weren't.

◆ Work with this chapter until you are totally free of all guilt.

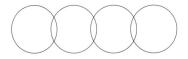

CHAPTER 12

END THE CYCLE OF CONFLICT

You can never have a cycle of conflict with only one person. It's impossible. Like a tennis match, two people are required to keep the cycle going.

The problem may seem to be the other person, but that's only half of the story. Both of you are resisting the other. Both of you are destroying love, and both of you are fueling the conflict.

While both of you are needed to create and maintain the cycle of conflict, only one of you is needed to end it.

To end the cycle of conflict, someone has

to take responsibility for the relationship. Someone has to stop playing the game.

If you want to end the conflict, you need to stop the resisting. You need to make sure the other person feels loved, accepted and appreciated. You need to make sure the person doesn't have to protect him or herself from you.

The moment you do this, the conflict begins to end. You start creating love instead of destroying it. By changing the way you treat the other person, you change the way that person treats you.

This is the key to restoring cooperation, but to be effective in making this change, you must first make a shift inside of you.

As long as you are full of upset and resistance, you will continue to fuel the conflict no matter how friendly you try to be.

So, to be effective in your relationship, you need to let go any resistance you may have towards the other person. To do this:

◆ Be willing to feel all your hurt. The avoidance of this hurt is what creates your resistance. Cry if you can. Let the hurt come and let the hurt go.

♦ Find the specific feelings of being worthless, not good enough or whatever else you've been avoiding. Let in the hurt of being this way. Remember that you are also the opposite.

♦ Accept the person exactly the way he or she is. Remember that acceptance is nothing more than surrendering to the truth. That person is the way he or she is whether you like it or not.

♦ Forgive the person. Forgive the person for not being wiser and more aware, and forgive the person for all the damage that he or she has caused. Let go of all your resentment.

♦ Take your full 100% responsibility for the loss of love in your relationship. Notice how non-accepting you were and notice how your actions have fueled the cycle of conflict.

♦ Don't hang on. Let the person go.

♦ Acknowledge the love that's still there.

To the extent you are able to let go of your resistance, you restore both your aliveness and your peace of mind. With the upset gone, you can then interact in a way that works.

After you let go of your resistance, the next step is to get with the other person and clean up your relationship. Do this in person if you can. If you can't, do it by telephone or by letter. Just make sure you do it.

This conversation is extremely important. This is the key to removing the other person's resistance towards you. This is what clears the past and lets the other person know that you are playing a different game now.

There are several primary elements to this conversation.

1. Take full responsibility for the loss of love in your relationship.

Tell the other person that you single-handedly destroyed the love in your relationship. Instead of making sure the person felt loved, accepted and appreciated, you were judgmental and critical. Tell the person that you did a lousy job of loving.

By your taking full responsibility for the situation, the other person no longer needs to be defensive around you, and the need to blame you begins to dissolve. This also makes it safer for the other person to take responsibility as well, and usually the person does.

2. Ask the person to forgive you.

Tell the person that you've made a lot of mistakes. Then ask the person if he or she will please forgive you.

Just by your asking, you move the person one step closer to forgiveness. Your asking can be very humbling for both of you. In most cases, the other person will be quick to forgive. Even if the person doesn't forgive, much of the person's resistance will disappear.

3. If you've been hanging on, give the person his or her freedom.

The more you try to control or hang on to someone, the more you push the person away. So let the person go. Be willing for the person to be gone from your life forever. By giving this person his or her freedom, you take away the person's need to resist you.

You can then put the focus on restoring the love, one human being to another.

END THE CYCLE OF CONFLICT

4. Tell the person that you love him or her and that you want to have your relationship work whether you are together or not.

Underneath all the hurt is the love. When you can acknowledge the presence of this love, it changes the way you relate to each other. You can then interact out of the love instead of the upset.

Make sure the other person knows that your relationship is important to you and that you want it to work whether you are together or apart. Tell the other person that you want to find solutions that work for both of you.

The purpose of this conversation is to end the conflict and restore the love, one human being to another.

Have this conversation as soon as you can. Your situation will begin to turn around as soon as you take responsibility for your relationship. You will probably notice immediate results.

After the conversation, make sure you follow it up with action. Use every interaction to make sure the other person feels loved, accepted and appreciated.

Remember, to end the cycle of conflict, someone has to end the volley of resisting, attacking and withdrawing from each other. It might as well be you.

EXAMPLE

Karen and Chuck had been in the process of a divorce for several years with no end in sight. Both were angry, frustrated, and quick to attack.

When Karen came to my office, she was desperate. The divorce was killing her. She had to do something to end the cycle of conflict. As we talked, she learned how to heal her relationship.

Her first step was to stop being so resentful towards Chuck. I worked with her until she was able to accept him, forgive him and acknowledge the love she still had for him. Once she did this, Karen was able to interact with Chuck out of her love instead of her anger and resentment.

The next step was to have her see that she was 100% responsible for the failure of her relationship and the conflict in her divorce. She needed to see that she was the problem, not Chuck.

Once Karen saw this, she could no longer blame Chuck for what happened. Although Chuck was also 100% responsible, pointing at him was useless.

As soon as Karen let go of her resentment and her blaming, she was in a position to meet with Chuck and clean up their relationship.

That night they met. Karen took full responsibility for what happened and asked Chuck to forgive her. She said she wanted to let go of the past and have their relationship be supportive. She told Chuck that she loved him and that she was committed to finding solutions that worked for both of them.

Karen took responsibility for what happened. Then she followed it up with action. She did everything she could to make sure Chuck felt loved, accepted and appreciated.

Chuck saw her sincerity and dropped his defenses. Although he was still cautious, fighting Karen became difficult. Within a few months, they resolved all their issues and were able to divorce as friends.

Karen ended the conflict the day she met with Chuck and took responsibility for their relationship.

ACTION TO TAKE

◆ Let go of any resistance you may have towards the other person. Work with this until you are totally at peace with the way the person is and what he or she has done. Be willing for the person to be gone from your life forever.

◆ Get with the person and clean up your relationship. Take full responsibility for what happened and ask the person to forgive you. State that you are playing a different game now and that you want your relationship to work whether you are together or not.

◆ Follow up your conversation with action. Take every opportunity to make sure the other person feels loved, accepted and appreciated. Remember that every action you take will either create love or destroy love and whatever you give will come right back.

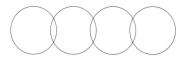

CHAPTER 13

REMOVE THE DISTANCE

Relationships usually start out great. People treat each other with love and respect. Then something happens and we get upset.

When you are upset at someone, you can't be with the person. There are a million miles of distance between you and the person you are upset with.

Before long, you get upset again and create more distance. Then you get upset again and create even more distance. As time goes on, the distance grows and the love gets buried, distance by distance.

Eventually, there is so much distance in

your relationship that you feel uncomfortable. It looks like you just don't love the person anymore, but the love that was present at the height of your relationship is still there. It's just buried by all the distance.

As this distance grows, you become defensive, critical and quick to anger. Upsets become more frequent and more severe. You create more and more distance. Soon the relationship that began as a dream turns into a nightmare.

This is the course of most relationships. They start out great and then go downhill. Then we get a new relationship and start the process all over again.

If you want to be effective in your relationships, you need to learn how to remove the distance. This is the key to maintaining love.

The most effective way to remove distance is to communicate your upsets. Say what you are upset about. Get it off your chest.

The moment you communicate your upset, the upset loses power. The distance disappears and the experience of love returns.

Look at the times in your life when you've

been upset and communicated it. Notice what happened to the upset after you got it off your chest. It disappeared. Now notice what happened to the distance. It disappeared as well.

Communication is the key to removing distance.

Unfortunately, we've been taught to communicate in a way that, instead of removing distance, creates more of it.

Instead of communicating for the purpose of restoring love, we communicate for the purpose of blaming, attacking, being right or changing someone.

The moment you do this, you put the other person on the defensive. That person then gets upset and has to fight to protect him or herself from you. Then you get even more upset. Without knowing, you fuel the conflict and create more distance.

You quickly learn that it's not safe to communicate your upsets. It's better to just keep them inside.

Well, the problem isn't in communicating your upsets, it's in how you do it.

If you really want to remove distance in your relationship, you need to communicate in a way that doesn't create more upset.

You do this by making sure your communication isn't threatening. Don't give the other person anything to resist. Make it safe for the person to hear what you have to say. Don't put him or her on the defensive.

Communicate for the purpose of removing distance and restoring love. Don't communicate for the purpose of blaming, attacking, being right or changing someone.

Take your full 100% responsibility for what happened and for your being upset about it. Don't blame the other person unless you want to argue.

The best way to communicate an upset is to find the hurt that's under your upset and communicate that.

Instead of saying "What's wrong with you? Why did you do that to me?" put the focus on your hurt. Say, "You did what you did, and I feel sad. I feel invalidated and I feel like you don't love me anymore."

Put the focus on yourself, not on what the

other person did.

Besides, it's your upset. When you blame the other person for your upset, you get to keep it. When you take full responsibility for your upset, you can let it go.

The question for you is this: What are you really committed to? Are you committed to removing distance, restoring love and having your relationship work, or are you committed to blaming, attacking, being right and changing the person?

The choice is yours. You can have resistance or you can have love. You can't have both.

If your commitment is to remove the distance and have your relationship work, there is a lot you can do.

You can start by finding the distance and removing it.

Distance is created by withholding something. Usually it's a bottom-line communication. "I'm angry that you didn't keep your promise," or "I'm sad that you don't love me anymore."

Once the communication is made, the

withholding stops. The upset is released and the distance disappears.

To find what you are withholding, imagine the other person being in front of you. Then look at what is between you and that person. What are you upset about? What is the distance?

Find what you need to say and then say it. Start from the beginning of your relationship and get everything said.

Before you start though, make sure you create an environment that's safe for communication. Make sure you let go of any resistance you may have towards the other person.

Then tell the person that there are some things that you want to say to remove the distance. Ask him or her to just listen. Then, say whatever you need to say.

If the person starts resisting you, stop and notice how you are communicating. You are either blaming or trying to change the person. Don't do that.

If the only way you can communicate an upset is by blaming, warn the person first so that he or she won't take it so personally.

Once you've said everything that you want to say, let the other person respond. Let the person say everything that he or she is upset about. Pull the upsets out.

The more the other person can release his or her upsets, the more that person will be able to express his or her love for you.

The key to removing distance is to get everything said. Get it off your chest. Just make sure the other person feels loved, accepted and appreciated in the process.

EXAMPLE

John was frustrated in his relationship with Sharon. He wanted to communicate his upsets, but every time he tried, Sharon would start arguing.

Communication seemed like a waste of time. So to avoid more conflict, John just kept his upsets inside. As the months went on, John and Sharon grew further and further apart.

After attending one of our workshops, John realized that he needed to change the way he communicated. He needed to communicate in a way that didn't put Sharon on the defensive.

So far, most of his communications had been some form of an attack. He would either blame Sharon for something or tell her she wasn't okay. Sharon would then get upset, become defensive and fight to protect herself.

To be effective, John needed to communicate in a way that wouldn't threaten Sharon. He needed to communicate for the purpose of removing the distance and restoring the love, not for the purpose of blaming, attacking or changing.

When he met with Sharon, he told her that there were some things that stood in the way of their relationship and that he wanted to get them off his chest. He asked her if she would please listen to what he had to say.

At first, this was very uncomfortable, but he continued. He told Sharon everything that he was upset about, but he did it in a way that made her feel safe. He didn't blame her for anything.

He said, "I'm angry that you keep spending when we don't have money to pay the bills. I hate it when I try to talk with you and you start arguing. I feel like you don't care about me anymore, and I'm sad about that. I miss your love and support. I miss being your friend." He kept the focus on himself and his feelings.

As John communicated his upsets and Sharon just listened, the upsets seemed to disappear. It was such a relief to get them said. Keeping them inside had been so painful.

After John said everything he was upset about, he gave Sharon an opportunity to do the same. As they continued to release their upsets, the distance in their relationship became less and less. The more they talked, the more they fell back in love.

By communicating his upsets and making it safe for Sharon to communicate hers, John was able to remove the distance in their relationship.

ACTION TO TAKE

◆ Make sure you communicate in a way that isn't threatening. Don't resist or attack. Don't blame or try to change the person. Make it safe for the person to hear what you have to say.

◆ Make a list of everything that stands between you and the other person. What are you upset about? What is the distance? Find the bottom-line communication for each upset.

◆ Then get with the person and communicate everything on your list. Tell the person that you want to remove the distance in your relationship and that there are some things that you need to say.

◆ After you have said everything you want to say, give the other person an opportunity to do the same.

◆ Make sure the other person feels loved, accepted and appreciated with every communication.

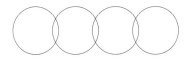

CHAPTER 14

RELEASE THE OTHER PERSON'S UPSETS

To remove the distance in a relationship, you need to release your upsets. You also need to release the other person's upsets. You do this by encouraging the other person to say whatever he or she is upset about.

Usually this is the exact opposite of what we do. Instead of encouraging communication, we discourage it.

We don't want to hear that people are upset at us. We don't like people pointing at our responsibility. We don't like looking at certain aspects of ourselves. We don't want to hear what people have to say. So we resist their communication.

We argue with people and tell them that what they say is not true. We tell them that they're wrong and that they shouldn't feel the way they do. Sometimes we even attack. We'll do anything rather than hear a communication that we don't like.

We act as though the person's upset will somehow disappear if we don't listen to it. Obviously, this doesn't happen.

If someone is upset at you, keeping the upset from being communicated certainly won't make it go away. Suppressing an upset only makes it worse. The upset gets stronger and now the person has a new upset for having been suppressed.

When someone can't communicate an upset directly, the upset will be communicated indirectly. The person may have an affair or just be resentful. One way or another, the upset will always be communicated.

It's much better to get an upset communicated directly than indirectly.

To the extent that you are able to understand and appreciate someone's upset, the upset loses power and no longer needs to be expressed.

Resisting a communication also produces more conflict. When you resist what some- one says, that person must then either sup- press the communication or communicate the upset more forcefully.

When the upset is said more forcefully, you feel threatened and resist even more. Then both of you become more frustrated and more upset.

This is what happens in any argument. Both of you are resisting what the other is saying. If either one of you would stop resist- ing and hear the other person's communica- tion, the argument would end.

The key to releasing someone's upset is to have the other person say whatever he or she is upset about. Let the person get the upset off his or her chest.

Ask what the person is upset about. Have the person tell you how he or she feels. Pull the upset out. Get it said.

If the person is ranting and raving, that's fine. It's much better to have the upset expressed than to have it kept inside. Keep pulling the upset out.

Listen to what the person has to say and listen to the communication from his or her point of view. You don't have to like what's being said or even agree. You don't have to do anything. Just listen.

"Yes, you are angry. You feel I let you down. You hate me. Yes, I understand. I don't blame you. Is there anything else?"

The communication may not be true, but it's true to the other person, and that's what counts.

The more you can appreciate and understand what someone is upset about, the more the upset disappears. It's just like taking the wind out of a sail.

By having the other person release his or her upsets, you can remove the distance and restore the love in your relationship.

EXAMPLE

Gene felt like Lynn hated him. No matter what he did, it was never enough. Lynn was always upset about something.

Then Gene discovered that he had made it almost impossible for Lynn to communicate. Whenever Lynn got upset, he would fight and argue. He would never let her say what she was upset about.

When Lynn couldn't communicate her upsets, she had to keep them inside. She felt suppressed and became more upset and more resentful.

Once Gene saw what was happening, he was eager to hear what Lynn had to say. He told her that he really wanted to know what she was upset about. He promised not to argue with her.

Lynn seized the opportunity and blasted him. She told him that she thought he was a loser and that she had no respect for him. She told him how angry she was.

It hurt to hear what Lynn had to say, but Gene continued to listen. He kept asking, "Is there anything else that you've been upset about?"

As Lynn expressed her upsets, they quickly lost power and disappeared. Lynn then became less defensive and more accepting of Gene.

Eventually, she explained how deeply hurt she had been by some things Gene said years ago. She had kept this hurt inside and had been protective ever since.

Once Lynn said everything she was upset about, Gene did the same. He told her how angry and hurt he was for not being accepted. He told Lynn all the things that upset him, but he made sure that he didn't blame Lynn or try to change her.

By the time both of them had said everything they could think of, their relationship had changed. The protectiveness disappeared and the intimacy returned. Gene and Lynn were closer than they had been in years.

By making it safe for Lynn to communicate, Gene released Lynn's upsets and restored the love in his relationship.

ACTION TO TAKE

◆ Listen to whatever the other person has to say, and listen from his or her point of view. Don't fight or argue. Just listen.

◆ Pull out the other person's upsets. Do whatever you can to have the other person say what he or she is upset about. Ask, "Is there anything else that you've been upset about?"

◆ If the person is ranting and raving, that's okay. Just keep listening and pulling out the upset. Remember that you don't have to like it or agree. Just listen.

◆ Make it safe for the other person to communicate anything.

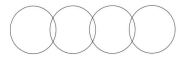

CHAPTER 15

BE WILLING TO FLOW

When a relationship doesn't work, we are often threatened with the loss of certain things that we don't want to lose; our children, our home, our security, our standard of living, and so on.

The moment you feel threatened with such a loss, you create a state of mind that actually increases the chances of your fear coming true.

You become so full of fear and upset that you lose your ability to see clearly. You get tunnel vision, and the only action you can take is some form of fighting, resisting and hanging on. This in turn destroys love and creates opposition and resistance against yourself.

For example, if you are threatened with the loss of someone, you will hang on to the person and push the person further away. If you have a fear of losing your children, you could deny the other person access and force him or her to fight for custody.

Literally, the more you fear that something will happen, the greater the chance that it will.

To be effective in handling your situation, you need to be free of the fear and the upset. You need to restore your peace of mind so you can see your situation clearly and so you can see what you need to do.

To learn how to be free inside, let's review what creates fear and upset.

Upsets seem to be caused by what happens, but they're not. Upsets are caused by your fighting and resisting what happens.

Select a recent upset and notice what would happen to the upset if somehow you were at peace with what happened. There would be no upset.

There would be no upset because the upset wasn't caused by what happened. The upset was caused by your fighting and resisting what happened. If you could somehow take away the fighting and resisting, there would be no upset.

Fear is similar to an upset, but instead of fighting and resisting what happened, you are fighting something that might happen in the future.

The more you fight and resist this future possible event, the greater your fear and the greater the chances are of your fear coming true. If you could take away the fighting and resisting, there would be no fear.

The key to restoring both your peace of mind and your effectiveness is to let go of the fighting and resisting.

To say this another way, you need to let go and be willing for anything to happen.

This may seem like a crazy thing to say, but this is the key to being effective in a difficult situation. This is also much easier said than done.

We don't want to let go because we don't want to feel all the feelings and emotion that would get reactivated if our fears were realized. This hurt from the past is what we are really avoiding.

To the extent you are willing to feel this hurt, the need to fight and resist disappears. You can then let go. You can restore both your effectiveness and your peace of mind.

To start the process of setting yourself free, make a list of all your fears.

What are you unwilling to lose? What are you unwilling to have happen? Are you afraid to lose your children, your home, your security or your standard of living?

Then, for each item, find the feelings and emotion that you are avoiding. What would you have to experience if your fear were realized? What would you have to face about yourself? Would you have to face the fear of being alone or of being not good enough or not worth loving?

Find what you are avoiding and then see if you are willing to face it. See if you are willing to feel all the hurt that would be reactivated if your fears came true.

Notice that your unwillingness to feel this

hurt certainly won't keep you from feeling it. Your unwillingness for something to happen won't keep it from happening.

Go down your list and work with each item until you are willing for all your fears to come true.

Remember, willingness is only a state of mind and is totally separate from your actions. For example, in your heart, you need to be willing to lose your children, but in your actions, do everything you can to make sure that never happens.

"Letting go" is the inner action that removes the fear and upset so that you can see what you need to do.

A powerful way to let go is to tell God or the universe:

"I now give you my children (or whatever you are hanging on to). I give you full permission to take them away. I want them to stay, but I let them go. I now release them forever."

Say this aloud and keep saying this over and over. Allow yourself to feel all the hurt that gets reactivated. Cry if you can. Keep saying this until you can say it and mean it.

Do this for every item on your list.

Then trust. Trust that no matter what happens, you will be okay.

Now trust doesn't mean that life will turn out the way you want it to. Life often doesn't. Trust is knowing that however life turns out, you'll be just fine.

When you know that you will be okay, no matter what happens, fear loses power and letting go becomes much easier.

So trust. Trust that you will be okay.

To the extent you are willing for anything to happen, you restore both your peace of mind and your effectiveness.

With the fear and upset gone, you see your situation very differently. You become creative and can discover solutions you could never have seen before.

Letting go and restoring your peace of mind is the key to creating a life that works.

EXAMPLE

Marilyn hung on to Robert until she eventually pushed him away. Then her biggest fear was that she would lose her children.

This fear was so strong that Marilyn became very protective. She did everything she could to keep the children away from Robert.

When Robert couldn't gain access to the children, he got upset. This threatened Marilyn and caused her to withhold the children even more. Eventually Robert had enough and filed for custody.

Marilyn's greatest fears were about to be realized.

When she came to me, she was terrified at the possibility of losing her children. The first thing I did was let her express all her fears and upsets. As she talked, she began to calm down.

Then I had her look at what would happen if she were to lose her children. What were her fears? What would she have to face?

As she looked, Marilyn saw that she hung on to her children for the same reason she hung on to Robert. She didn't want to face her fear of being alone and of not being loved. This was what she was really avoiding.

I then asked her if she was willing to experience all the hurt of being alone and of not being loved. I worked with her until she was.

Once Marilyn faced her fears, she was no longer threatened by the loss of her children. She didn't want to lose them, but she knew that if she couldn't have them, life would continue and she would be fine.

The moment Marilyn let go of her fear, she changed her relationship with Robert. She let him be with the children as often as he wanted. When Robert saw that he could have all the access that he wanted, he dropped his fight for custody.

By letting go of her children, Marilyn was able to keep them.

ACTION TO TAKE

◆ Make a list of all your fears. List everything that you are not willing to lose or that you are not willing to have happen. Notice that your unwillingness won't keep your fears from coming true.

◆ Work with your list until you are willing for each item to happen. Remember that "willingness" is only a state of mind and is totally separate from your actions.

◆ If you have difficulty letting go of something, look to see what you would have to confront or experience if that fear were realized. Be willing to feel the loss and the hurt. Cry if you can.

◆ To let go of something, tell God or the universe, "I give you full permission to take this away forever. I want it to stay, but I let it go." Say this over and over, until you can say it and mean it. Allow the hurt while you repeat the words.

◆ Trust that no matter what happens, you will be okay.

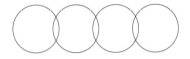

CHAPTER 16

RESOLVE DISPUTES
WITHOUT CONFLICT

In every divorce, there are certain issues that need to be resolved. Decisions need to be made about the care and support of the children. How will the debts and the property be divided?

How you go about resolving these issues is extremely important. It determines the type of divorce you have and it sets the stage for how your relationship will be in the future.

Normally we handle these questions in a way that causes tremendous damage. Here's what usually happens:

Two people start out being in love. Then someone gets hurt. Then that person puts up his or her walls of protection and automatically withdraws and becomes critical of the other.

Then the other person gets upset and becomes more judgmental toward the first person.

Without knowing, the couple creates a cycle of conflict that goes on and on without either person ever noticing his or her role in the problem.

The suffering that comes from this conflict is painful enough, but as soon as you add the threat of losing your children, your financial resources and your well-being, the situation quickly becomes much worse.

Now the situation is threatening. This potential loss of well-being can be a serious threat to a person's survival. It can make a person fight as though his or her life depends on it.

The moment this happens, the cycle of conflict escalates dramatically. Often this conflict escalates into full scale war. People become so full of fear, upset, anger and resentment, that they do horrible things to each other.

The hurt and destruction are enormous. Relationships are destroyed and financial resources are lost. The pain and suffering are often so great that people never recover.

The sad part is that none of this conflict and suffering is necessary.

We believe that we have to fight to protect ourselves. We think that if we just fight hard enough, then somehow, everything will get resolved in our favor, but this doesn't happen. In fact, the opposite is true.

The more you fight someone, the more of a threat you become to that person. You then force that person to fight you even harder. This in turn puts you at even greater risk.

Everything you do as an adversary creates more adversariness against you and makes your situation worse.

Besides, when all the fighting is over, the issues that you fought so hard to win rarely get resolved the way you want them to. In most cases, the issues get resolved in some sort of compromise with no one being happy.

The final solution is one that could have been worked out between the two of you with a lot less effort and a lot less expense.

The key to resolving issues without conflict is to stop being a threat to the other person. Be committed to finding solutions that are fair and that work for everyone.

When someone is committed to everyone's well being, the adversarial process stops. How can you fight someone who's on your side?

As a matter of physics, adversariness requires two opposing forces. When one opposing force is removed, the adversariness disappears. It takes two people to be adversaries. It only takes one person to stop it.

As soon as you draw sides against someone, you create an opposing force. So don't draw sides. Keep your focus on finding solutions where everyone wins. This is the key to resolving issues without conflict.

When you focus on everyone's well-being, you create an environment of cooperation and understanding. You can then work together to find solutions, and when you look for solutions, you find them.

This is how you resolve issues. You find solutions.

This makes perfect sense, but as crazy as it may seem, in an adversarial situation, there is no focus on finding solutions. None. All the focus is on winning.

When there is no focus on resolving issues, they don't get resolved. Trying to resolve issues in an adversarial situation is like playing tug-of-war. It takes forever to accomplish anything and every step is full of effort and struggle.

In most contested cases, the people are so caught up in the fighting that they don't even know what the issues are. It's insane. So keep your focus on finding solutions.

Look for the other person's fears and concerns. Look beyond what the person is asking and find what the person needs.

For example, the real issue behind most custody cases is the fear of losing the children. When you can insure easy access and broad visitation, the fear loses power, and so does the need to fight for custody.

If the issue is child support or alimony, you can find what the court would do and agree to that.

If you can't come to an agreement, use the

services of a mediator.

Whatever the issue, there is a way to resolve it. Sometimes you find the answers quickly. Sometimes you don't. Just make sure you don't quit.

Finding solutions that work for everyone also includes you. A commitment to everyone doesn't mean that you have to give up your soul in the name of cooperation. You don't have to be taken advantage of.

Sometimes you need to be careful. Some people are dishonest. Sometimes you need to say "no." Sometimes you may need to go to the judge.

Do whatever it takes to have find solutions that work for both you. Just don't lose sight of your commitment to everyone's well-being.

Even if the other person demands everything and refuses to cooperate, don't draw sides. As difficult as your situation may seem at the moment, it can get much worse.

Keep looking for solutions that work for everyone.

The type of divorce and the type of relationship you have is determined by how you treat the other person and how you resolve your differences.

You can keep your pride, draw sides and go to town on each other; or you can be committed to a relationship where everyone comes out ahead.

The one you choose will affect the entire rest of your life.

EXAMPLE

Brad and Carol were in the process of divorce. Brad wanted to part as friends, but found it very difficult. Carol was very demanding. She wanted to receive unreasonably high child support, most of the property, and none of the debts.

She didn't care about Brad's welfare, and when she didn't get what she wanted, she became abusive.

Brad's, natural tendency was to fight. He wanted to declare war, pay her nothing, and seek custody of the children. This situation could have very easily turned into a nightmare.

Fortunately, Brad was more interested in the welfare of the children and his future relationship with Carol than he was in being an adversary. He continued to work with Carol and do whatever he could to heal their relationship.

He also said "no" whenever he felt it was appropriate. When Carol got mad, he let her be angry, and he still said "no." He didn't attack her or even draw sides against her. He kept looking for solutions that worked for both of them.

Eventually their relationship began to heal, but Carol's demands remained unrealistic. Instead of considering her demands as an attack, he respected her different opinion. He just didn't agree.

When it became apparent that they would never reach an agreement, Brad asked for the judge to decide. Even at the courthouse, Brad refused to say anything bad about Carol.

When the trial ended, the judge did almost exactly what Brad had initially offered. Carol didn't like it, but she no longer blamed Brad.

Since they never became adversaries, there were no battle scars and no resentments. Once the divorce was over, the relationship healed quickly. Brad saw his children often and developed a close, supportive relationship with Carol.

Brad's refusal to draw sides against Carol avoided an almost certain war. He was able to say "no" without putting Carol on the defensive. He was able to resolve their issues in a way that allowed their relationship to heal. He kept the peace.

ACTION TO TAKE

◆ Notice how your demands and actions have been threatening to the other person. Notice how you have forced that person to protect him or herself from you.

◆ Refuse to draw sides against the other person. Don't be adversarial. Don't be a threat.

◆ Look at the situation from the other person's point of view. Look for that person's fears and concerns.

◆ Be committed to finding solutions that work for both of you. Keep looking for what it takes to resolve the issues. Don't give up. Be willing to flow. Be flexible. Work together as much as you can.

◆ If you can't come to an agreement, use the services of a mediator.

◆ Find solutions that work for you too. Be willing to say "no" when appropriate.

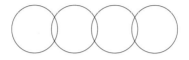

CHAPTER 17

HAVE YOUR ATTORNEY
WORK FOR YOU

There are countless individuals who have gone to an attorney for an uncontested divorce only to have it become contested overnight.

Our society is adversarial, promoting the unconscious notion that whenever there is a dispute, sides have to be drawn. One side will then end up on top and the other on the bottom. To make sure you are not the one on the bottom, you need to fight to protect yourself.

This is what most of our attorneys have been taught. They believe that the best way to take care of their clients is to fight for them.

When these attorneys look at divorce, all they see is the warfare that is all around them. When they look at this condition, it seems obvious that people have to fight to protect themselves.

They don't notice that the condition they observe is their own creation. This warfare is created by their own adversariness, and we demand it.

As a culture, we don't notice the hurt and suffering that is created by an adversarial system. We don't notice the damage that it does to relationships and to people's well-being.

Adversariness may have been needed at some point in time, but now it's outdated. Now we can take the focus off of winning and direct our efforts toward finding solutions that work for everyone. It is far more important to be a peacemaker than to be an adversary.

Whenever an attorney is committed to ending adversariness and furthering everyone's well-being, he makes a very special contribution to the world. He minimizes conflict, resolves issues and promotes the healing of relationships. He makes the world a better place for all of us.

This type of attorney is truly needed. If you are going to get a divorce, look for one like this.

Unfortunately, there aren't very many of them. Fortunately, their numbers are growing rapidly. If you find one, you will bc in good hands.

Usually, attorneys that do divorce mediation tend to be less adversarial.

If you can't find a non-adversarial attorney, you will have to do the best you can.

Stay out of the legal system as much as you can.

Select an attorney. Have him file the petition and start the waiting period. Get all the legal advice and information that you need. Find out what questions need to be resolved. Then go home and resolve them.

When you have an agreement that works for both of you, take it back to the attorney. Let him review it and do the paper work.

To the extent that you are able to resolve these issues by yourself, the legal process will go quickly. When you let adversarial attorneys resolve your issues, you are asking for trouble. Your case can go on forever and cost a fortune in legal fees, not to mention the cost in well-being.

If you are already deep in the legal process, it's never too late to turn your situation around. Get in communication with the other person. Clean up your relationship and take responsibility for the situation. Start working together to resolve your issues.

If your attorney makes your job more difficult, let him go. After all it's your relationship, not his. The more you resolve your own issues, the easier your life will be.

Sometimes the other person is so dishonest or uncooperative that a stronger attorney is essential. If this happens, make sure that your attorney takes care of you. Just don't let him be too adversarial.

When an attorney takes an aggressive action against someone, it's like an attack. Sometimes the attack is like Pearl Harbor. He may have taken the action, but you are the one who gets the blame. You are the one who has to suffer the consequences, not him.

Like it or not, you are responsible for what your attorney does. You are the one that hired him and you are the one who pays his fees.

Make sure your attorney knows that his job is to forward your relationship and to find solutions that work for everyone. Have him watch out for your interests, but don't let him attack.

Remember, your attorney works for you. You don't work for him. If he is unwilling to work with you in this way, find an attorney who will.

The system of adversariness continues because we demand it. We want to come out on top. We want to get even. We want to fight.

Now there is a new opportunity. Now we can focus on creating peace and harmony in the world and in our hearts. It's the only thing that really matters.

When you divorce as good friends, you make an impact on the planet. You make it possible for more couples to do the same. You show it can be done.

It's something worth accomplishing.

EXAMPLE

Peggy and Mitch decided to go their separate ways. There were no hard feelings, they just didn't get along well together. They wanted to part as friends.

Peggy would have custody of their two boys and keep the house. Mitch would pay the mortgage and $900 a month in child support. They had it all worked out.

When Mitch went to file, his attorney said he was about to give away too much. When he told Peggy he wanted to pay less, she got upset and decided to see an attorney.

Her attorney said she was about to be taken advantage of, and to protect herself she needed to obtain temporary orders from the Court. This would cost $3,500.

Peggy then closed out their savings, paid the attorney and served Mitch with papers ordering him to appear at a hearing.

When this happened, Mitch felt personally attacked. It not only violated his understanding of their agreement, but now he had to borrow $3,500 to protect himself. Furious, he then canceled the credit cards, demanded title to the house, and paid Peggy the minimum child support necessary.

Peggy and Mitch declared war on each other before they knew what happened. Now they were spending thousands of dollars in attorney's fees with no end in sight. They lost control of their own divorce.

Fortunately, they started talking again. They saw that they had created a monster, and now they wanted to end it.

They realized that is was their relationship and that they were going to resolve their own issues. They got all the advice they could and stared working on an agreement. When they finished, they took it back to their attorneys. They got some more advice and made some more changes.

When Peggy and Mitch were both satisfied with all the terms, they had their attorneys prepare the final paperwork and finish the divorce.

The legal nightmare ended when Peggy and Mitch decided to use their attorneys as advisors instead of adversaries.

Ironically, after all their revisions, the final

decree was almost identical to their initial agreement. By resolving the issues themselves, they were able to get out of the courthouse and get on with their lives.

ACTION TO TAKE

◆ If you need an attorney, find one who is non-adversarial. Attorneys who practice divorce mediation tend to be more supportive.

◆ Stay out of the legal system as much as you can. Use attorneys as advisors, not as adversaries.

◆ Get all the legal advice you can. Then work with the other person to resolve your issues. When you have worked out all the details, take your agreement to the attorneys and let them do the paperwork.

◆ Don't let your attorney attack the other person or make your situation worse. Remember, you pay the consequences for whatever your attorney does.

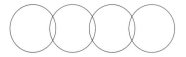

CHAPTER 18

IT'S UP TO YOU

What we want most is to have peace on our planet, peace in our lives, and peace in our hearts. This is what we want, but we live in a way that makes this almost impossible.

Instead of being accepting and appreciative, we've been taught to be judgmental and critical. Instead of taking responsibility for our lives, we've been taught to blame and to resent.

Without ever knowing, we destroy love, both in our relationships and in our lives. We create resistance and opposition against ourselves. We create tremendous suffering, and none of it is necessary.

It is possible to live in the experience of love. It is possible to have love in all your relationships and in every aspect of your life. However, to do this, you need to adopt a new way of living.

You need to learn how to flow with life and to be more accepting and tolerant of others. You need to forgive and to heal your hurt.

Put your focus on well-being. Have it be more important to be free inside than to win, to be right, and to get what you want. Put your focus on finding solutions that work for everyone.

Open your heart and express your love.

When you live your life in this way, opposition melts. You create an environment of love and support. Life works for you instead of against you.

This is the key to being effective in life, but to make this happen, you need to do some work. You need to be committed to creating a life of love.

Remember, every time you interact with another person, you will either create love or destroy love, and whatever you give will come right back.

If your situation looks tough or seems impossible, don't quit. Keep giving love. Follow your intuition and keep taking the next step. Then take the next step and the next one. Keep your focus on the result you want and keep taking the next step.

Eventually, your situation will clear up and you will be fine.

The only thing that can get in your way is your pride and ego.

You have a choice. You can either live out of your pride and ego, or you can do what works. You are the one who has to live with the consequences of whatever you choose.

It would be great if the other person would play the same game, but you certainly can't wait for that. If you want your life to be great, you are the one who's going to make it happen.

It's up to you.

This is a book that you will want to read over and over. Every time you read it, you will discover more about you, your relationships and your life.

If you want to handle your situation quickly, have a telephone consulting session with Bill Ferguson or a member of his staff. For more information, call 713-520-5370.

If you want to learn more about love and how to create a life that works, read our other books and listen to the audio tapes. If you are on the internet, visit www.billferguson.com or www.divorceasfriends.com.

Thank you and
I love you.

Bill Ferguson

HEAL THE HURT THAT RUNS YOUR LIFE

Discover And Heal The Inner Issues That Destroy Love And Sabotage Your Life

This book is also available on audio cassettes.

Paperback, 120 pages

Every one of us has an inner issue that destroys love and sabotages life. What is your issue? Is it failure, not good enough or not worth loving? As you discover and heal this hurt, you profoundly change the way you live your life. Fear and upset seem to disappear. You become free inside and able to see life clearly. You become creative and far more effective. This life-changing book will show you how to find and heal this hurt.

ISBN 1-878410-21-0   Paperback $10
ISBN 1-878410-22-9   Two Audio Cassettes $16

MIRACLES ARE GUARANTEED

A Step-By-Step Guide To Restoring Love, Being Free And Creating A Life That Works.

Paperback, 160 pages

This book shows, step-by-step, how to have love in every aspect of your life. You will learn how to find and heal the issues that run your life and sabotage your dreams. You will learn how to take charge of your life and be free of upset and stress. You will discover how to clean up your life, find your life purpose and experience your spirituality. This profound yet simple book covers every aspect of living in the light.

ISBN 1-878410-20-2 Paperback $11

HOW TO HEAL A PAINFUL RELATIONSHIP

*And If Necessary,
How To Part
As Friends*

**This book is also available
on audio cassettes.**

Paperback, 156 pages

In this unique book,
Bill Ferguson shows,
step-by-step, how to remove
conflict and restore love in any
relationship. You will learn what creates
love and what destroys it. You will discover how
to end the cycle of conflict, heal hurt, release
resentment and restore your peace of mind. Bill's
experience as a former divorce attorney provides
rare insight into the nature of relationships. You
will discover something about yourself and your
relationships that will change your life forever.

ISBN 1-878410-25-3   Paperback $12
ISBN 1-878410-24-5   Two Audio Cassettes $16

HOW TO DIVORCE AS FRIENDS

Four Audio Cassettes

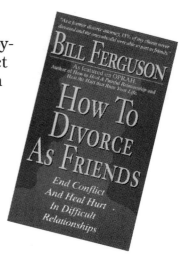

These tapes show, step-by-step, how to end conflict and restore cooperation in even the most difficult relationships. You will learn how to heal your hurt and be free of guilt and resentment. You will discover how to resolve issues quickly and effectively. You will learn how to part as friends.

Tape 1 - End The Cycle Of Conflict. Learn how to end conflict and restore your peace of mind.

Tape 2 - Heal Your Hurt. Find and heal the inner issues that create your pain and sabotage your life.

Tape 3 - Clean Up Your Relationship. Be free of guilt, anger, resentment and blaming.

Tape 4 - Resolve Issues Peacefully. Learn how to resolve your issues without conflict.

ISBN 1-878410-24-5   Four Audio Cassettes $25

THESE AUDIO CASSETTES WILL HELP YOU DISCOVER MORE ABOUT YOU, YOUR RELATIONSHIPS AND YOUR LIFE.

Set yourself free & enjoy your life

This album includes each of the following 8 audio cassettes for only $65.

Individual cassettes are available for $10.

ISBN 1-878410-01-6 $65

How To Love Yourself

- Be free of self-invalidation.
- Release the issues that run your life.
- Love yourself just the way you are.

ISBN 1-878410-02-4 $10

How To Have Love In Your Life

- Discover what creates love.
- Learn how to communicate effectively.
- Have love in all your relationships.

ISBN 1-878410-03-2 $10

How To Be Free Of Guilt And Resentments

- Be free of all anger, resentment and guilt.
- Restore your inner peace.
- Have difficult relationships work.

ISBN 1-878410-04-0 $10

How To Be Free Of Upset and Stress

- Be at peace in any circumstance.
- Release the mechanisms that keep you upset.
- Restore your piece of mind.

ISBN 1-878410-05-9 $10

How To Create Prosperity

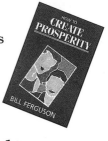

- Release the mechanism that creates lack and financial stress.
- Remove your blocks to prosperity.
- Learn how to create abundance.

ISBN 1-878410-06-7 $10

How To Create A Life That Works

- Discover how you create your own unworkability.
- Be free of the hidden actions that sabotage you.
- Learn how to clean up your life.

ISBN 1-878410-07-5 $10

How To Find Your Purpose

- Earn a living doing what you love.
- Have your life make a difference.
- Discover your life purpose.

ISBN 1-878410-08-3 $10

How To Experience Your Spirituality

- Connect with your life force.
- Experience being one with God.
- Discover the Light.

ISBN 1-878410-09-1 $10

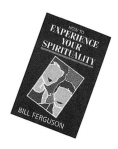

SPIRITUALITY: TEACHINGS FROM A WORLD BEYOND

Two audio cassettes

Several years ago, some profound teachings were received through a form of meditation. Since then, thousands of people have had their lives deeply altered. Through these teachings, you will discover the essence of spirituality. You will exper- ience a oneness with God and will discover a truth that will profoundly alter your life.

ISBN 1-878410-11-3 $16

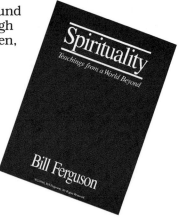

TO ORDER BOOKS AND CASSETTES

Item		Price	Qty	Amount
How To Heal A Painful Relationship	Book Audio	$12 $16		
Heal The Hurt That Runs Your Life	Book Audio	$10 $16		
Miracles Are Guaranteed	Book	$11		
How To Divorce As Friends 4 Audio Cassettes		$25		
Set Yourself Free This album includes each of the following 8 audio cassettes		$65		
• How To Love Yourself	Audio	$10		
• How To Have Love In Your Life	Audio	$10		
• How To Be Free Of Guilt And Resentment	Audio	$10		
• How To Be Free Of Upset And Stress	Audio	$10		
• How To Create Prosperity	Audio	$10		
• How To Create A Life That Works	Audio	$10		
• How To Find Your Purpose	Audio	$10		
• How To Experience Your Spirituality	Audio	$10		
Spirituality: Teachings 2 Audio Cassettes		$16		
Subtotal				
Texas residents add 8% sales tax				
Shipping and handling: Add 10% of Subtotal $4 minimum, $8 maximum				
Total				

Name (Please print)_____

Address _____

City_____

State _____ Zip_____

Telephone Day (   )_____ Evening (   )_____

For MasterCard or Visa orders only:

Card No. _____ Total $_____

Exp. Date_____ Signature _____

Send your order along with your check or money order to:

Return to the Heart, P.O. Box 541813, Houston, Texas 77254
For Telephone orders Using MasterCard or Visa call (713) 520-5370
www.billferguson.com • www.divorceasfriends.com

If you want to have a telephone
consultation with Bill Ferguson or a member
of his staff, call us at
(713) 520-5370.

You can find us on the internet at
www.billferguson.com
www.divorceasfriends.com